Defensive Investing

Published under licence 2017 by Searching Finance Ltd.

ISBN: 978-1-907720-21-5

Typeset and designed in the UK by Deirdré Gyenes

Printed in UK by Searching Finance

Defensive Investing

Investing and Managing Risk in a Trump and Brexit World

Walter Marlowe

About the author

Walter Marlowe has been an active investor in both the US and UK stock markets for over 40 years. He was a banker in the US, the Netherlands and the UK for over 30 years with experience in corporate banking, private equity and leveraged debt.

He has also worked extensively in bank consulting in Europe and the Arabian Gulf privately and in association with BankTandD Consulting, London and has taught and lectured on private equity, bank strategy and investment strategy at City University, London and Boston University Graduate Business School, London and for a number of banks and training consultancies.

Mr. Marlowe was born in New York City and has an MBA in banking and international finance from New York University's Stern School of Business.

The author and his wife Maureen live in London and on the U.S. east coast. They have two daughters and two grandsons all of whom live in the Los Angeles area.

Questions and comments can be directed to him at wamarlowe@aol.com

About Searching Finance

Searching Finance publishes books on economics, finance, politics and history. Visit *www.searchingfinance.com*

Contents

Chapter 1
Introduction

As this book goes to publication in the first quarter of 2017 we have Brexit in the UK (and its eventual impact on Europe) and we have Donald Trump and his cabinet nominations of plutocrats and climate deniers. Politics aside, reflecting on last year, we started 2016 with a major market "correction" and a reasonable chance of heading into a genuine market crash. But post January and through April we experienced a rally in market indices only to be followed by an extended "sideways" trending market (almost always bad news for individual investors).

We now have a post-Trump rally based on the "rumor" of his economic stimulus plans with the real possibility of an imminent reversal based on the "news" (the economic and fiscal realities) relating to those stimulus plans (an old stock market adage: "buy on the rumor, sell on the news" (meaning the outcome of the rumor).

There remains a wide spread belief that Trump or no Trump, Brexit hard or soft, we're heading over the next two to three years to a major market crash which is being signaled by several historic indicators of market trouble. A number of commentators and perhaps more ominously, several major equity investors, are on record predicting a crash more severe than the years 2000 and 2008.

The timing of any major market move is really unknowable as is its probable severity but, what is known is the extremely parlous state of the global financial system and the problem is not just centered in Italy or in Britain with Royal Bank of Scotland. The global financial problem extends from the US banking system's exposure to sub-prime auto loans to Deutsche Bank's capital inadequacy to China's out of control official and non-official parallel banking systems. The multi-trillion dollar derivatives exposure of the world's handful of "too big to fail" - systemically critical banks is undoubtedly the critical core of a failing structure.

The uncertainty and the volatility experienced (or perhaps "suffered") by investors is why Defensive Investing can make a lasting difference in terms of wealth generation and wealth preservation.

As a "Defensive Investor" I'm leaning heavily to the crash school of opinion. I have money but no ego invested in this matter and was happy to close my short positions, take my profit and switch tack. But I continue to believe that global monetary and economic trends are against us over the next several years and caution is critical.

My market pessimism is based on a particular reading of the economic fundamentals. I don't think the developed economies are really improving and thus paving the way for market gains. Government statistics suggesting an economic recovery are tenuous and carefully selected and interpreted for the popular press.

Moreover, as an investor who is mindful of market technical issues, I think it's very concerning that the major US and UK market averages are within inches of diving through their 200 day moving averages. If this "support point" is pierced and remains so for several days to weeks that is a very dependable, oft repeated, sign of continuing market woe.

Even in the current uptrend the major global market indices are still in dangerous territory and the current rally of two months stands a very good chance of just being a "bear market rally" – a short term rally in a long-term bear market.

This book is about managing risk as a Defensive Investor. We have now entered into a market environment where Risk Management for the sake of capital conservation is critical for the typical, middle class, private investor – in other words, you, the reader, and me, the author.

Who should read this book and why

Defensive Investing and portfolio management for the "common man" is a highly pragmatic and very "doable" investment philosophy, strategy and process. This book is aimed squarely at so-called "retail" or individual investors. It does not matter if your personal investment portfolio is $40,000 equivalent or $4 million equivalent. If you want to manage all or part of it, or if you are required to at least agree investment categories or asset allocations with your broker, wealth manager or pension fund manager (corporate or private), this book is for you. Neither the value of your portfolio nor your level of "engagement" in making investment decisions matters; this book will still be of significant use to you while hopefully also being an engaging read. The size of your capital or your place in the decision-making process doesn't matter in terms of relevance for two reasons:

1) Warren Buffet's investment rules:

Rule 1: Don't Lose Money;

Rule 2: Remember Rule 1.

2) When you review the performance of your wealth manager, broker, or pension fund manager and you complain that it is anywhere from unsatisfactory to miserable, you can be sure they will blame you for the asset allocation choices you made, the risk tolerance level you indicated to them, or the market. And, no, they won't be rebating your fees or compensating you, as it wasn't their fault.

This book is all about practical disciplines and investment processes for private investors with an emphasis on capital conservation and risk management. Investing can be fun and challenging and intellectually satisfying. Losing your capital along the way and failing to reach financial independence, particularly in your later years, is not "fun".

This book posits "conservation of capital" as a first principle. Lots of investment advisors and analysts advocate this basic concept. Conservation of capital isn't fun – it's work. It's not macho and it's not exciting, but after you have experienced couple of big hits to your capital and as you get ever older, it becomes an ever more valid preoccupation.

If you read the news (and as a Defensive Investor you have to) then you know by now that neither banks, nor central banks and governments, nor Wall Street or the City of London have your interests at heart. If you think they do, stop reading now – you're not going to benefit from this book.

What is Defensive Investing?

It is:

- An investment philosophy and as such it is based on a set of values and a set of "rules". Rules help guide decisions so that they are congruent with values.
- An investment strategy – and as such it has a set of goals and a process for achieving those goals.
- An investment process – and as such it has a set of mechanics for realising / facilitating the strategy to achieve its goals.

The processes are reasonably simple, straightforward and eminently achievable by any investor today, given the tools available on the Internet and particularly online broker trading platforms.

Defensive Investing – the goal

Defensive Investing (and this book) has one simple goal: achieving financial independence.

My father (and Don Vito Corleone, the Godfather) both advised their sons not to become "puppets on a string". Financial independence is relative. It is whatever amount of capital you need / will need with respect to your circumstances, values and interests to be as independent as possible of the government, Wall Street and an employer for your long run financial security.

Why? Because governments have and will need to reduce social benefits such as retirement plans in the future. Wall Street exists for its own benefit, not that of investors, and your employer pension fund can either go broke or, more likely, be downgraded from a "defined benefit scheme / final salary plan" to a "defined contribution plan" (or in extreme – have to be rescued by a government pension protection plan and your benefits reduced as part of the bail-out). As things now stand you largely have to *contribute your money and take your chances on the future value of stock and bond markets.*

Financial independence is being free of soul-destroying anxiety as you approach the end of your working life.

Defensive Investing – the values

To quote the title of a book by Gerald Loeb investing is 'The Battle for Investment Survival'. Loeb is a distinguished old-school investment analyst whose excellent and still in-print book is worth reading. It is a battle to conserve capital, manage risk and grow capital over time. I didn't believe it was a battle when I first read Loeb in the 1970s, but I do now. With regard to Wall Street / the City of London versus the private investor, I urge you to read Paul Farrell and David Weidner on the internet for a clear understanding from market professionals and veterans of the 'battle for investment survival" the forces arrayed against you.

Not everything on Wall Street or in the City of London is against you, the private, retail-sized investor – not everything, but almost everything, and that is a big part of the battle. The other factors are our emotions, our delusions and a failure to focus on realistic goals.

The core values of Defensive Investing are, to borrow a term I learned as a Classics major at New York University, "syncretic"; that is, we freely borrow principles from other investment philosophies where relevant, appropriate and valid.

- **We buy value** – we focus on stocks that are fairly priced and not hyped and almost always stocks that pay dividends at levels well above inflation
- **We invest in Themes,** also known as thematic investing; this is discussed in Chapter 2. These investment ideas form the "Core" portfolio" of "Core and Satellite" portfolio structure, which is discussed in depth in Chapter 4. Our key Theme is value and a subsidiary theme is buying things people really need and which have tangible, real value. A Theme is a focused, logically coherent idea that exhibits certain characteristics that we believe creates value and generates attractive returns over time.
- **We manage risk to conserve capital**. We don't run big losses or let our losses run. Setting stop losses (or stops) post an investment decision is not a separate exercise; it is step two of a two-step purchase process. Stop losses are a price you set at which you will sell, either automatically or by choice and that greatly reduce the risk involved in trading shares. Stop losses are discussed in Chapter 3.
- **We stay alert and focused on our goals**. Warren Buffet says he never looks at stock prices. The late John Templeton, another world champion investor, said to

always track stock prices. We can split the difference. Having set our stops, we can review our investments daily, twice weekly, weekly. Whatever frequency is comfortable for us and which we will consistently do.

- **We maintain intellectual curiosity and intellectual openness.** Defensive Investing requires you to read and be aware of socio-economic, political and politico-economic news and trends, to think those news items and trends through and relate them to your circumstances, goals and investment position. Intellectual openness means not just listening to yourself or like-minded investors / analysts. Always take time to read contrarian views and then consider them objectively.
- **We act consistently but we are open to changing our positions based on information.** Consistency of action is not rigidity. I had a bit of a crisis during the summer of 2011 because of market events. A lot of my core investment beliefs were challenged, severely. It took me a while to work through that conundrum and do so logically and coherently. I changed some of my Defensive Investment principles in the face of "new information", new understandings. We evolve or we die. John Maynard Keynes, who is not much in fashion right now as an economist, was an accomplished investor. Once challenged for changing his opinion on a topic, he famously said: "When the facts change I change my opinion. What do you do?"

Defensive Investing – the rules

1) As per Benjamin Graham (Warren Buffet's mentor and the dean of value investing) and Buffet, and as previously mentioned: Rule 1: Don't Lose Money; and Rule 2: Remember Rule 1.

2) As per John Maynard Keynes: The market can remain irrational longer than you can remain solvent. Don't be rigid – be alert and be open to change
3) Economics is not a science, it is a social science. Investing is not a science; it is also a social science because, just like the economy, capital markets are driven by human behavior and human interaction. Equity markets are, like their participants (humans) highly imperfect; to populate those markets and to paraphrase Sergeant Friday of 'Dragnet' fame (Jack Webb): "We have to recruit from the human race."

Key points

In conclusion, I want to stress a few key points about Defensive Investing that will matter to you, the reader.

- Defensive Investing is, as I mentioned above, "syncretic"; it has elements of several different investment philosophies and strategies. The point is not to be blazingly original here, it is to construct an investment process can work and be executed by private investors. The product of over 40 years as an investor, this book includes many of the strategies, risk management tools and disciplines used by successful professional investors. The strategies are not difficult to understand or implement; the risk management tools are very easy to understand and implement, but they do require discipline on your part
- This book is not a "tip-sheet" and it is not a mechanical, 10-minutes-a-week, fail-proof investment process. It is not based on any algorithms or any great discovery of market anomalies we can all exploit in our spare time when not trawling Facebook or Linkedin.
- You need to be aware of the world around you and you need to follow that information flow, consider it

and then think how to apply it in terms of investment themes and decisions.

- Defensive Investing is investing for the long haul, and as such and without exaggeration, it is entirely possible for the non-professional investor to replicate professional fund manager results over time. Sebastian Lyon, a very successful UK fund manager who runs the Trojan Fund, has benefited in great part from the fact that the fund was seeded (started up) using the family money of a well-known British industrialist, Arnold Weinstock. The Weinstock family did not interfere with Lyon's management of the fund once it delegated it to him. He did not have to worry about redemptions or investing irregular and sometimes cumbersome new inflows of money, and importantly, the agreed investment horizon was long-term.

You may not have Lyon's particular analytical or stock-picking skills, but you have many of the same advantages he had that allowed him to take sensible decisions over long investment periods. You are managing your own money and you to not have to compete with other managers or deal with clients.

About this book

I am very interested in the equity market and in great part it is the intellectual content and challenge that attracts me. I have an MBA, I was a corporate finance banker and I have been a private investor for 40 years.

However, the point of this book is to be a pragmatic guide to what I think is a coherent, achievable strategy for a wide range of investors.

From time to time, some of the theory of the market (the intellectual content) will be explored because it will either help elucidate some key points or it will help to convince you of the wisdom of those points.

The book contains a number of excerpts from equity newsletters and magazine articles that will help explain the Defensive Investing process with material examples. Also, I hope reading somebody else's prose will help you to better understand mine.

I have included information about information sources I think you will need to and want to investigate and possibly use. I have no financial arrangements with any of these market information and opinion providers. I am often a paid subscriber to what I recommend and that is the full extent of my relationship. I think these information sources are genuinely useful. They will be your most convenient and objective source for staying abreast of the investment markets and critical socio-economic trends. It is this kind of wholly accessible information that many of your fellow non-professional investors use that greatly increase their abilities as investors and improves markedly their investment experience and returns. You can do the same.

Walter Marlowe
London, Los Angeles June 2016

Chapter 2

The Core Portfolio – Themes and how to Identify, Evaluate and Exploit Them

In Chapter 4 we'll discuss portfolio construction and the methodology I advocate for a Defensive Investor – Core and Satellite portfolio construction. The foundation of Defensive Investing is the construction of the Core portfolio. This is the component of your total equity portfolio that is going to have the greatest weighting. That weighting can and will vary over time and in accordance with market, political, socio-cultural and economic circumstance. The weighting can range from, for example, 25%, to over 50% of your equity holdings or more depending on your circumstances and genuinely felt preferences.

Investment Themes

The Core component of our total portfolio is our "high conviction" positions. There's more on Conviction Investing in Appendix 2. This is the portfolio which is going to combine both growth and defensive characteristics and it involves the selection of investment "ideas", Themes, that we believe are going to give us significant capital appreciation over time but also incorporate critical defensive characteristics.

Themes are the product of our views about key social, political and economic trends. But they are also going to reflect our principal beliefs about what constitutes growth with value and resilience. This doesn't mean and cannot mean that the Theme will never have downtrends or be out of "market fashion". It is a search for what the American Nobel Prize winning author, William Faulkner, described as things that will "endure and prevail". Not an easy task and certainly subject to subjectivity.

For the sake of conservation of capital, it may be necessary for us to "rotate out" of our Core portfolio or to reduce its weighting or "hedge it". Simple "Buy and Hold" investment strategies may work over long periods of time, which is why it worth maintaining a long-term set of core holdings. But we need to flexible and open-minded in our approach. Overall, so-called "Buy and Hold" investing has not worked well over time when we aim to buy and hold a whole portfolio of stocks. Buy and Hold has worked very well if we can pick an exceptional stock – IBM in the1940s, Microsoft, Google, Berkshire Hathaway. But, these are really exceptional stocks and, given the size of the stock market universe, they are really few and far between (and please note that in the "infant" stages few investors saw any long-term worth in them).

Over the last decade, as a result of increased market volatility and repeated "crashes", Buy and Hold has been widely refuted and discredited. Against this view looms the specter of Warren Buffet, the ultimate Buy and Hold investor. Buffet is a great stock picker, using a very stringent set of investment criteria and he has of course succeeded mightily. Unfortunately, lots of Buy and Hold investors have not been able to replicate his success. Buffet has a number of advantages we don't have, not the least of which is timing. Buffet has benefited from the longest and most pronounced bull market in history. He also has a very large and varied portfolio and he, or his holding company Berkshire Hathaway, actually manage some of their key businesses, such as in the insurance sector. Additionally, the size of his investable capital makes it possible for him to cut some exceptional deals when he is prepared to take apparent risks (e.g. helping to bail out Salomon Brothers, support Goldman Sachs and other transactions).

I'm not refuting Buy and Hold. I am saying it has to be intelligently and unemotionally managed.

By way of a footnote to Buy and Hold: a number of analysts have calculated rolling 20-year returns for the major market indices such as the Dow and S&P 500. What the analyses have shown is that timing can be critical. For example: a 20-year rolling return starting in 1929 presents, not surprisingly, dire results. The same is true for a 20-year rolling return starting in 1966. These results contrast markedly with a 20-year rolling return starting in, say, 1979.

The point to be made here is investing and then "forgetting" for the long haul can have some very unhappy returns. Market events and timing can undo your retirement plans. Active monitoring and rebalancing is critical.

Buy and Hold strategies

You will often see statements about the market and investing which may assert, for example, that $1,000 invested across the Dow Jones Index in 1920 would be worth several million dollars today by virtue of a simple Buy and Hold strategy.

This is not true. It might be true if you put all your money into say, IBM, but not if you had allocated your $1,000 evenly across all the index components. Why?

All market indices have what is called a "survivor's bias", meaning that companies in the index that eventually fail or fall below the market measure used to determine index inclusion are dropped from the index and the index is recalculated such that the effect of these "non-survivors" disappears.

Had you been an investor in one or more of these companies that were dropped from the index you would have continued to feel the effect in terms of diminished real investment capital and need to make up those losses.

Buy and Hold, particularly over longer periods of time, requires you to keep "rebalancing" – dropping unsuccessful stocks and replacing them with successful stocks.

The only way a 90-year long Dow buy and hold strategy would have worked without rebalancing is if you had bought a Dow Index fund and let the fund manager do the heavy lifting of rebalancing. Unfortunately, such funds didn't exist back in 1920.

Themes defined

The term "Theme" and the construction of a "Themed portfolio" can be a broad definition and a broad undertaking. I am defining Themes in a more restricted manner.

The defining words that I want to emphasize in describing a Theme are: dominant, recurrent and distinctive. Let's keep this in mind as we go along; it's a framework we want to maintain and within which we want to operate.

There is something that a certain type of hedge fund manager does that we also want to do as Defensive Investors and that is most specifically in the identification and management of investment Themes.

The type of hedge fund I'm talking about is called a Global Macro fund, which is a fund that follows a so-called "global macro" investment style.

Global Macro investing

Simply stated, a Global Macro fund can invest in any kind of asset anywhere in the world where the fund managers think there is an opportunity to make an attractive return on a risk-adjusted basis. There are probably around 50 to 60 major Global Macro fund managers around the world.

Successful managers don't wander aimlessly around the globe looking for a random investment idea. In many instances the managers come from specific trading and investing backgrounds and may have expertise in certain areas such as energy trading, for example, which then becomes a focus. Most importantly for us, they also follow a process and a discipline that we can and will want to follow.

Typically, Global Macro managers start out with what some of them call "reference scenarios". Reference scenarios are similar to our Themes. They're a type of "big picture" idea about the global economy, economic trends and political and social trends.

(Those of you who have read the book or seen the film "The Big Short" will readily understand what I'm getting at. The principal investor protagonists in the book, Burry and Baum, identified a theme, a reference scenario – critical distortions in the US home ownership / mortgage origination markets.)

Generally, these reference scenarios are the product of fundamental, conventional economic thinking and observation. They are not quantitatively derived; they are not based on inside information. They are the product of awareness, research and to some inevitable degree, intuition. Intuition is often the starting point. Intuition is a product of awareness of the social, economic and political environment we live in.

Intuition in this instance is the sensing that something is unique, like John Paulson, among a few others (cited above) did in sensing that the sub-prime mortgage market was a mess, was fundamentally flawed and could only end in tears.

Armed with a reference scenario (or simply read, Theme) Global Macro managers try to validate the scenario and then look for specific investment ideas that fit into those reference scenarios or Themes. They analyze those opportunities and do so to ensure that the investment idea conforms to their convictions. If, after analysis and reflection, the idea seems valid, it can become an investment.

The Harvard historian Niall Ferguson has said that what impressed him about the Global Macro investors he met was: "...the way they proceeded from theoretical insights ... to empirical research to the conception of a particular transaction to the execution of the transaction ..." Given that this process also describes how an historian moves from an hypothesis, to a thesis, to research, to a book, it's not surprising that Ferguson was impressed.

We're going to do this same thing, but unlike hedge funds with their often substantial research capabilities, we're going to do it in a way that we can manage with the resources we can bring to the job.

The Global Macro reference scenario process is the antithesis of making snap trading decisions. It's laborious and it can generate a lot of legitimate overhead (those unpaid interns have to sit some place!). But seriously, folks, as old-time comedians used to say, it is detail and it can be time-consuming. When your investment size is a couple of hundred million dollars or pounds, the research effort is neither costly nor wasteful of time on a relative basis (relative to the money you're investing and hope to make).

But what about us – those investors somewhere short of $100 million to punt with. Is the effort worthwhile? The answer must be yes, because whether we are talking about a $10,000 or £100,000 investment, it is our capital and once lost, we've got a problem. Our goal, in addition to capital conservation, is capital growth and our task is to find how to accomplish both goals simultaneously.

According to an article written by James Shinn for *Institutional Investor* magazine:

- Global Macro funds use stop losses to manage their risks (stop losses are among the techniques which we will use – see Chapter 3).

- Global Macro funds are very aware that unexpected events can undermine their strategies and lead to investment losses and knowing that, they both review their ideas and portfolios on a regular basis; they use stops as noted above to manage risk, and they listen with open minds to people with viewpoints other than their own.

- A key risk that every investor faces both on a company-specific level and on a market-wide level (so-called "systemic risk") is "events". Harold Macmillan, British prime minister from 1957 to 1963, once counseled a young colleague that the principal political risk he and his party (the Conservatives) faced was "events, dear boy, events". A prime example of a market moving "event" would be, for example, something that significantly impacted energy prices, such as Saudi Arabia falling to Islamic extremists, or even the shale oil and gas boom ongoing in the USA. There are lots of potential company-specific "events" that can have severe and lasting impact on a company's operations and share price.

As this book goes to publication we are experiencing a huge energy market "event" – precipitated by the success of oil and gas fracking in the US, petroleum oversupply globally resulted in the Saudis deciding to over-produce oil in order to put US independent oil producers out of business and hence recapture oil market share and eventually boost petroleum prices back to a level that works for Saudi Arabia.

Another example: a London Stock Exchange listed small company called Rurelec is a developer and operator of small-scale electric generation projects in Latin America. The company had good management and good operations and it served a growing market with excellent fundamentals ... except the political aspect. Its Bolivian operations were unexpectedly nationalized by the Evo Morales government and compensation has yet to be agreed. The company's share price collapsed and has yet to recover.

Developing a Theme into an investment

I want to look at two potential Themes – genuine "Global Macro" type investments that we can all understand and relate to and we can all evolve into specific stock market investments. However, right now I think one of the Themes is demonstrably stronger than the other based on market returns and prospects. Both Themes appear equally compelling and valid, but one Theme appears to be more vulnerable to "events" than the other. The contrast hopefully will demonstrate the care that needs to be taken in committing to a Theme – making a Theme manifest in terms of investment.

Theme One – We're getting old but living longer

I think you can agree with me that this Theme is well researched, strongly supported in terms of evidence, "Big", in terms of size and consequences and easy to grasp and understand. Is it "foolproof"? No. Is it free of "event risk"? No. But so far in investment terms it has "legs" and should continue to do so, with inevitable ups and down due to both company- and sector-specific and market systemic risks.

The Theme is all about demographics, mainly in the well-to-do Western developed world, but increasingly also in those major developing economies that are producing a widening middle class and wealth class.

The Theme is simply about the goods and services an increasing older, longer-lived and relatively well off population will need and want. We are talking about: medical services, medical instruments, hospitals, retirement homes, retirement services, pharmaceuticals, biotechnology, medical insurance, companies that market to "over 50s" –marketing everything from health insurance to home insurance to auto insurance to vacations tailored to seniors.

The target population is growing and growing in both economic and, importantly, political influence. This Theme has already proved out its investment validity, having provided very high levels of current income (dividends) and capital appreciation for investors. There is every reason to believe, to have the conviction and to a high level, that this Theme will continue to run, providing both appreciation and a good measure of inherent capital conservation.

Some examples of investment targets for the Theme, in both the US and UK: "Big Pharma", biotech companies, hospital companies and care managers, biotech funds and ETFs. Specific names in both the US and UK: Pfizer, Astra Zeneca, Bristol Meyers, Gilead, Teva, Shire, Glaxo, Saga, McCarthy and Stone, Target Healthcare REIT, Medicx, Smith and Nephew,

Stryker, Private Health Properties and many others easily searched out in internet stock screens.

Are there risks? Certainly. Biotech companies without portfolios of established drugs are like oil and gas explorers without producing wells. Big Pharma companies are politically vulnerable and are increasingly finding it harder and harder to develop new drugs, in-house, efficiently. All drug and medical device companies are subject to regulatory problems and potentially large lawsuits.

The entire health and retirement industries are dependent on government welfare programs to buy their drugs, pay nursing home fees, provide adequate government medical plans for their populations, and adequate pension arrangements. Going forward, there is a lot of genuine concern about the ability of governments to maintain these programs at anything near current levels and the inadequate retirement provisions being made by large segments of the population in all Western societies.

In the UK many smaller companies supplying goods and services to the NHS are often negatively impacted by minor (and major) changes in NHS procurement policies and budgets. On the other hand we can cite, again in the UK, companies that have mightily benefited from NHS policies such as those funds that buy and build modern standard general practitioner offices for NHS GPs.

The same is true in the US with regard to Obamacare and the policies and behaviors of the medical insurance industry, those companies that provide "managed care" services and the crisis facing a number of municipal employee pension and health plans.

The Theme is strong, not risk-free and subject to potentially huge changes over time. But for now, however long "now" proves to be, this is a proven and powerful Theme. And as with all Themes care has to be taken as which investment opportunities are used and how the risk inherent in all investments is managed.

For contrast I want to choose another very compelling and I think easily understandable Theme that has not proven out in terms of providing consistent returns.

That Theme is Food & Agriculture.

Theme Two: We're getting bigger (more populous) and hungrier

Validating the Theme

Without belaboring the point, people need to eat and will necessarily reduce expenditure on every other item, discretionary and non-discretionary (e.g. shelter) in order to feed themselves and their families. This is a given and certainly a strong starting point for a Theme.

In opposition to the point above, in the developed world, food is a commodity in the fundamental sense of the word and that is not itself a really strong starting point for an investment Theme.

But let's dig deeper.

- With the exception of Brazil, around the world, including the western world and China, the volume and quality of arable land is contracting due to development, pollution, environmental change and poor farming practices.
- World population has literally gone hyper-geometric and is doubling at a genuinely frightening rate.
- The emerging world is becoming ever more able to afford more and better quality food (e.g. palm oil production has benefited mightily from this trend in India, China, Latin America and Southeast Asia), and in doing so is actively competing with the West for food.
- Akin to food & agriculture, let's add in to the Theme water resources (for agriculture as well as direct consumption). We know the issues with water resulting from pollution, population growth, environmental

change, such as drought, extreme weather incidents and seemingly changing weather patterns around the world and increased industrial use of water, including bottled water, other beverage production and industrial processes such as shale fracking.

- The globalization of agricultural trading and its impact on resource allocation, pricing and industry trends (e.g. the increased privatization of key agricultural / agri-business resources (i.e. grain trading and the buying and long term leasing of developing country arable land by wealthier nations such as Saudi Arabia and China)). Globalization increases and facilitates demand and the satisfaction of that demand (actual consumption) also contributes to the reallocation of resources based on price and it contributes to the volatility of food prices.
- The growth of agri-business and its extension into new growing areas such as the Mato Grosso and the Amazon in Brazil. Agri-business changes production, distribution, input consumption and pricing patterns. It consolidates resources and production into fewer more powerful hands (economically and politically).

Food & Agriculture (and its critical components and inputs such as water and fertilizer, seeds and pesticides) are clearly dominant, recurrent and distinctive as a Theme. How valid is this Theme? Let's refer back to the trends / factors / issues that we set out above. And again, we all have to eat.

Until governments start producing "Soylent Green" (Google the reference!) we are entirely dependent on agriculture (including fish farming).

Our validation process doesn't stop at the conventional and obvious wisdom that we all have to eat. We have to determine if there is a valid investment case; what would that investment case look like; what would it be influenced by; how can we access it; and if we can access it, does it still work for us as so-called portfolio investors (not majority owners or managers). We are atomistic investors. Our personal participation doesn't influence the investee company or the industry.

I think the points we set out above demonstrate that there is clearly a valid investment case. We know that factors such as climate and climate change, government policy (for better and worse), wars, population growth and population shifts, agricultural science and global politics will all impact the Theme in both positive and negative ways.

Looking over those potential influences on our Theme, almost all of them point to higher food prices and higher input prices going forward. Global politics and government policy can be disruptive (e.g. price controls, nationalization of resources, etc.), but historically, most governmental intervention only exacerbates problems, leading to shortages and higher prices. (For example, US legislation on mandatorily adding corn-based biofuel to gasoline drove up global corn prices and lead to hunger and street demonstrations around the developing world, including the USA's semi-stable neighbor, Mexico).

Science in general and agri-science in particular has mitigated the Malthusian syndrome, fortunately. We don't want human misery and don't need scarcity to validate the Theme. Agri-science itself creates products and investment opportunities we can exploit.

Accessing the Theme

Taking into account the points made above there are several aspects of the overall Food & Agriculture Theme that we can access as investment propositions:

- We can take a 10,000 feet above the ground view and invest in Food & Agriculture Exchange Traded Funds (ETFs) (see Chapter 7); and we can invest in commodity specific ETP's (exchange traded products) – the later option I deem as not at all appropriate for non-specialist traders

- We can also achieve diversification by investing in a Food & Agriculture fund (unit trusts or investment trusts) (also discussed in Chapter 7);
- We can focus on companies that produce:
  - Farm machinery
  - Fertilizers
  - Seeds and pesticides;
- We can invest in companies that own and hold land for food production (as well as forestry and development);
- We can invest in food processors and traders;
- We can invest in food producers and food component producers (e.g. corn syrup, palm oil, sugar, other edible oils, animal feedstock, etc.).

Now, let's take a look back at the performance of various food and agricultural investments.

Principal agricultural stocks – recent performance

As of May 2016

	1-year price change (%)	5-year price change (%)	P: E ratio	Dividend yield (%)
Agrium	−14.3	26.0	12.3	4.4
Archer Daniels	−18.6	10.0	13.2	3.06
BASF	−23.1	6.9	16.2	4.12
Bunge	−30.9	−20.4	12.2	2.56
Deere	−6.8	−13.0	15.1	2.91
Dupont	−2.9	26.0	30.5	2.3
Monsanto	−20.6	42.6	29.5	2.3
Syngenta*	21.7	29.4	27.0	2.75

* Being acquired by ChemChina (which had a major positive impact on the 1 year price change)

Courtesy of Investors Chronicle

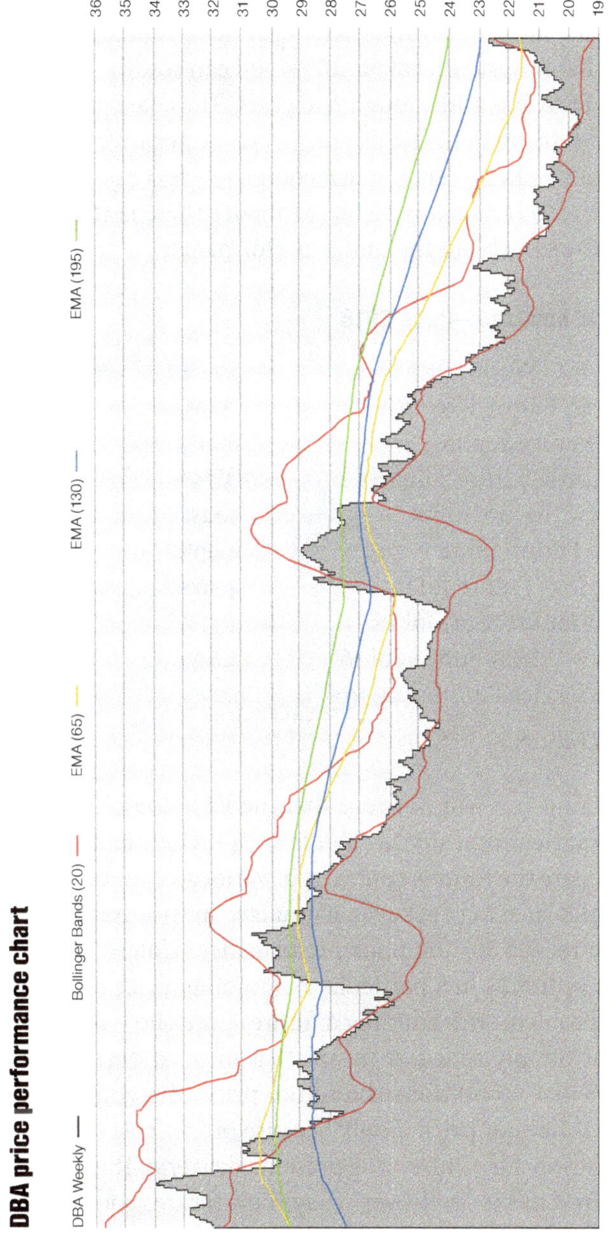

Chart courtesy of BigCharts.com

The above chart is a five-year chart running from June 2011 – June 2016 for the agricultural exchange traded fund, DBA, the Deutsche Bank Agricultural Fund. As you can readily see from the chart, DBA has had a tough five years. The chart pattern is particularly strong in that it displays a classic negative pattern; repeated "lower highs" set out in a completely text book classic pattern. On top of this terrible performance there isn't even as dividend to smooth out the under-performance.

DBA's top 10 holdings – June 2016

1	Sugar #11 (World) Oct 16	7.74%
2	Soybean Future Nov 16	7.19%
3	Corn Future Sep 16	6.21%
4	Live Cattle Future Aug 16	5.75%
5	Coffee 'c' Future Jul 16	5.12%
6	Cocoa Future Jul 16	4.99%
7	Lean Hogs Future Jul 16	4.50%
8	Wheat Future(Cbt) Jul 16	2.71%
9	Kc Hrw Wheat Future Jul 16	2.60%
10	Cattle Feeder Future Aug 16	1.77%

Courtesy ETFdb.com

The first thing you will notice is that the ETF doesn't contain any of the agricultural stocks cited in the previous table. What it invests in are the futures contracts of various key agricultural commodities such a corn, sugar, wheat etc. The portfolio structure is the reason for the poor performance. Unless we have consistent uptrends in a particular commodity price there is a technical problem with running a futures portfolio – it's called "contango". Simply stated, it means that in most periods and under "normal" conditions the future price of a commodity will exceed the spot price if only because of the "cost of carrying" a position for future, not present, delivery. This means that the Fund has to "roll-over" (buy) new futures contracts at higher prices than realized on expiring contracts (an expiring contract becomes the "spot" or current price) – getting less in proceeds and paying more to extend the exposure to a particular commodity contract is not a winning formula for a Buy and Hold investment fund. For investors to benefit from this type of ETF, they have to "trade it". They have to buy into short-term price trends and sell out as the trend wanes.

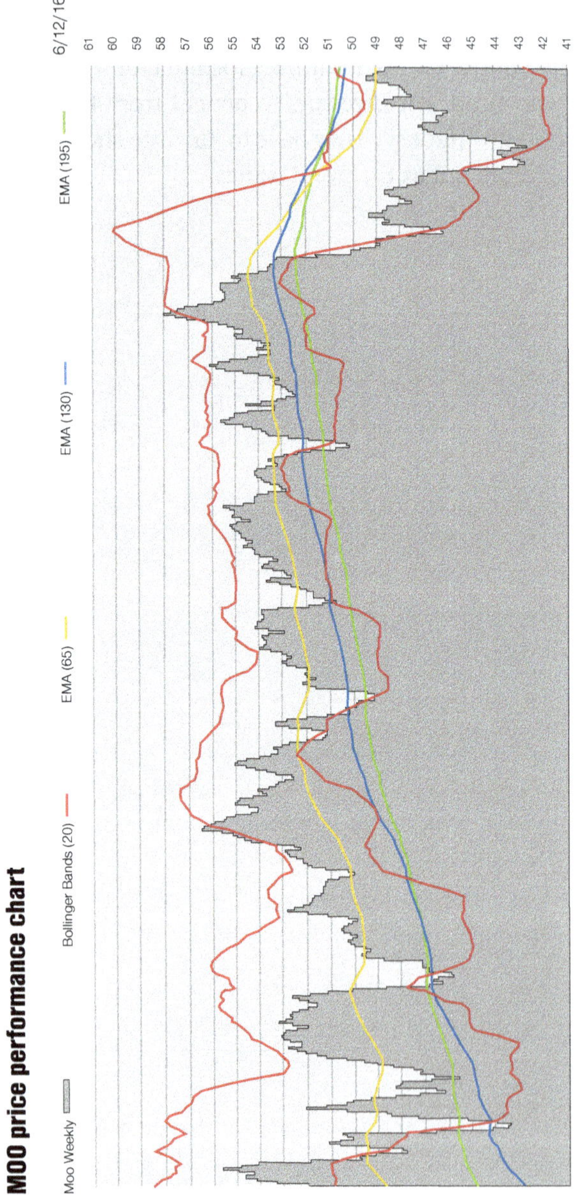

Chart courtesy of BigCharts.com

The chart above is for an ETF colorfully named "MOO". Again it's a five-year chart running from 2011 to 2016. Its top 10 holdings as of June 2016 consist of:

MOO's top 10 holdings – June 2016

1 MON 9.73% – Monsanto Co
2 SYT 7.39% – Syngenta AG ADR
3 ZTS 7.26% – Zoetis Inc
4 ADM 6.83% – Archer-Daniels Midland Co
5 DE 6.66% – Deere & Co
6 KUBTF 5.15% – Kubota Corp
7 TSN 5.09% – Tyson Foods Inc Class A
8 POT 3.72% – Potash Corp of Saskatchewan Inc
9 TSCO 3.61% –Tractor Supply Co
10 AGU 3.60% – Agrium Inc

Courtesy ETFdb.com

With MOO we have an ETF that invests in agri-business stocks. You can see from the chart that MOO's performance over the period is also very disappointing. As with DBA, there were a lot of "tradeable" moments over the period, but as a Buy and Hold investment, even for periods as short as a year, it was not a rewarding investment. It's also worth noting that the chart is almost book-ended by similar deep lows.

The point of all of this is simply that while Food & Agriculture sounds like great investment Theme underpinned with very strong fundamentals, the reality has been dramatically different from the predictions of so-called "modern Malthusians". This doesn't mean that the concern of modern Malthusians as to how we will feed even a modestly growing world population in the face of climate change, the loss of arable land, and the loss of clean water isn't a genuine issue; it's just as an investment Theme it simply hasn't played out to date.

Just to elaborate on the point a bit, below is a five-year chart for a UK international water and power ETF – Ecofin Water and Power Opportunities. The fund invests globally in listed water and power companies in both the developed and developing worlds. As you can see, apart from its blip in 2015, the fund has gone literally nowhere over five years.

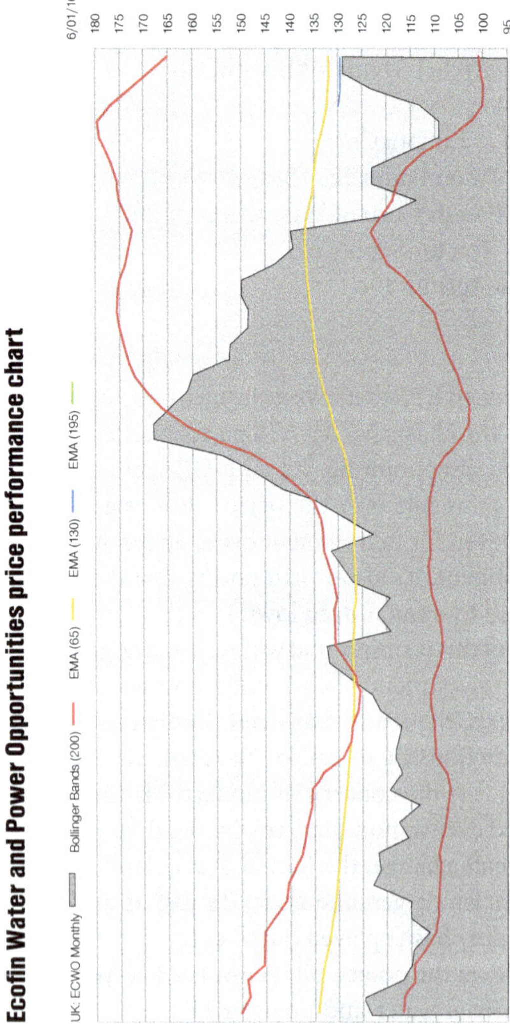

Chart courtesy of BigCharts.com

Just to complicate things a bit, look at the below five-year chart for a US company called American Water Works.

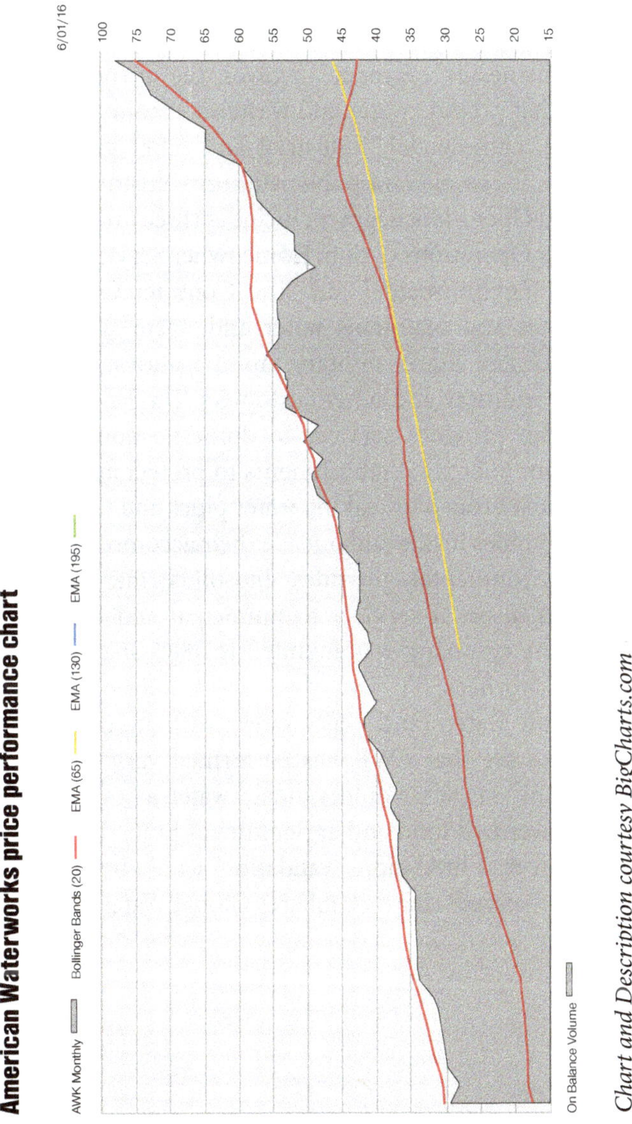

Chart and Description courtesy BigCharts.com

Company description

American Water Works Co., Inc. provides water and wastewater utility services to residential, commercial, industrial, public, and other customers. It operates through two segments: Regulated Businesses and Market-Based Operations. The Regulated Businesses segment involves the ownership of subsidiaries that provide water and wastewater utility services to residential, commercial, industrial and other customers, including sale for resale and public authority customers. The Market-Based Operations segment includes three lines of business: Contract Operations Group, Homeowner Services Group and Terratec Environmental Ltd. The Contract Operations Group operates and maintains water and wastewater facilities for the United States military, municipalities, the food and beverage industry and other customers. The Homeowner Services Group provides services to domestic homeowners and smaller commercial establishments to protect against the cost of repairing broken or leaking water pipes and clogged or blocked sewer pipes inside and outside their accommodations. Terratec Environmental provides biosolids management, transport and disposal services to municipal and industrial customers. The company was founded in 1886 and is headquartered in Voorhees, NJ.

Focusing on water (and wastewater) without the power sector you can see that AWK has performed very well over the period. This in part would validate water as opposed to water and power and food and agriculture as potentially valid Theme. However, a little more "validation" would be helpful.

Below is a five-year chart for iShares Global Water ETF.

iShares Global Water ETF price performance chart

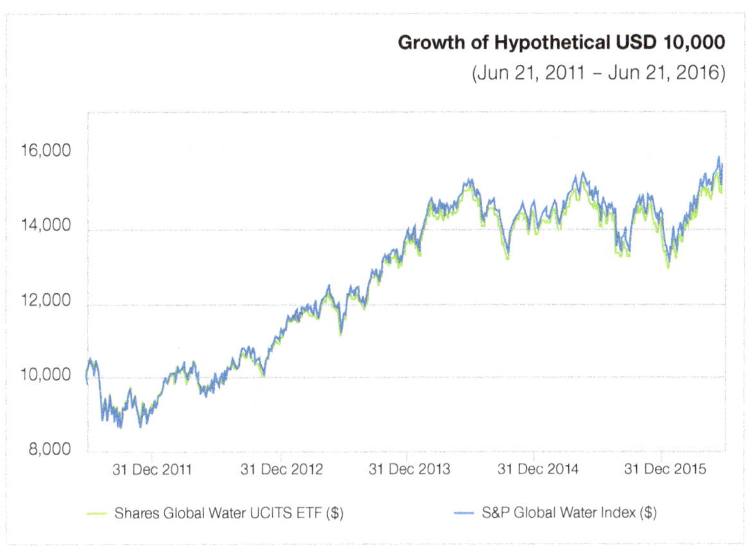

Below we have the chart for Powershares water ETF.

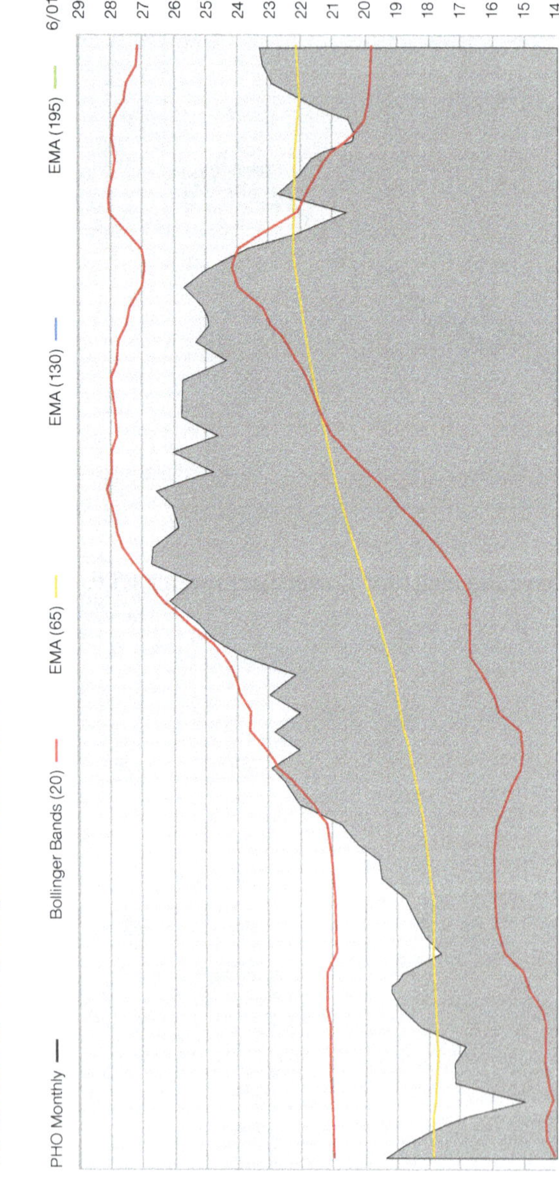

Chart courtesy of BigCharts.com

A lot of charts: what's the "take-away". Firstly, sectors / Themes that ought to be correlated from an intuitive point of view (Food & Agriculture and Water) aren't always positively correlated. Secondly, when looking for a "point of access", a fund or share to invest in to facilitate a Theme, it really pays to do some extra research. Mixing power and water in an ETF was not a winning formula and did not provide diversification benefits for water investors. There are a number of structural, markets and regulatory reasons for the divergence in Water shares performance and Food & Agriculture shares performance. A little research, not an onerous amount, can quickly highlight the key differences:

1 Food is a genuine commodity and agriculture is notably impacted year on year by weather issues, government subsidy issues, over-production and the action of big producers and traders and futures markets.

2 Water is a regulated industry and is no longer a commodity, and pricing trends have begun to recognize the scarcity issues surrounding clean water.

3 Water provision tends to be in the hands of larger companies which can "stabilize" supply and price.

4 Water is not transported over the distances that agricultural products are, and this further helps to stabilize the supply side of the business.

5 Water is not traded on futures markets and hence those markets don't have knock-on effects on spot prices, as is the case with food.

Returning to the use of Themes in the construction of Core Portfolios

Set out below is a discussion of the mechanics involved in this process.

Differentiating among and choosing access points

Once we've targeted a Theme and have been able to identify multiple points of investment access e.g. individual companies of interest, funds and ETFs. Assuming we want to proceed with an involvement in this Theme, what decisions do we now need to take; what preferences do we need to express?

1. **Investment size:** The amount of your investable capital that you would allocate to any one Theme and then to investments within that Theme is a matter of Risk Management and it is always a trade-off between your enthusiasm and commitment to a Theme and the management of risk through diversifying your positions and limiting your exposure to any one position.

   We will discuss this at greater length in the Chapter 3, Risk Management. There are several issues to consider and lots of rules of thumb and processes that can be used to set risk : reward parameters. Your investment in any Theme and your sub-allocation of that investment into specific assets will be determined by your Risk Management preferences and process.

2. **Risk and risk concentration:** Having taken an overall view on the risk : reward equation of the Theme (determining and evaluating risk : reward ratios is explored in a later chapter) the matter at hand now is how best to structure and manage that trade-off. For example:

   a. If you felt that the overall risk of the Theme was greater than your core comfort level on investment risk, you would then seek to manage and defray some of that

Theme-based risk (or "category risk") by making more diversified, more conservative asset selection choices – in other words more diversification, more stock selections and less concentration.

b. Within the Theme of a growing aged population you could mitigate risk by investing in a selection of health care and pharmaceutical mutual funds (unit trust) or an ETF or investment trust that either "indexed" the sector or was "actively managed" by stock selecting within the sector. By choosing either instrument (and we will discuss the different instruments in Chapter 7) you:

    i. Have selected a "composite" investment that is diversified to a greater or lesser degree within the Theme. As I believe most readers will know, diversification is good in terms of reducing risk and improving risk-adjusted returns;

    ii. If you have selected an actively managed fund (one that does not simply index the entire sector but selects stocks and manages its positions to conserve capital and heighten returns) then you may benefit from the quality, professionalism and diligence of the manager(s) who can provide a level expertise well beyond our own.

c. Some research on the assets you are considering will give you a reasonably good idea about historic risk and return of the various investment instruments you are considering and some services such as Morningstar rate funds and you can use their star and risk ratings as the basis for choosing investments and determining how much of the Theme investment money you want to allocate to each individual investment.

3. **Performance issues:** Comparing performance, set out below are charts for some of the potential Theme investments.

I could have used precious metals, most specifically gold as the illustrative investment choice for a different Theme. As many of you know, gold prices have risen by circa 600% since the year 2000. The chart for the Gold ETF (GLD) looks very dramatic particularly when overlaid against the Dow – see below.

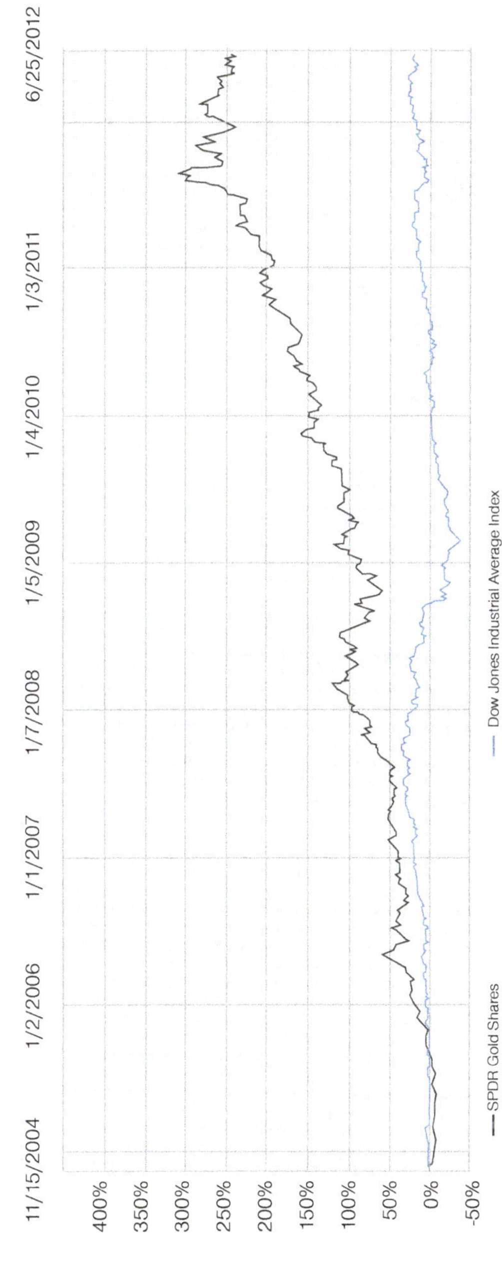

Chart courtesy of MSN Money

Gold was a very valid and powerful investment choice as a particular Theme over the period shown in the above chart. Gold, in any form, bullion, coins or the ETF, could have been the access, the investment instrument for the Theme of the global debasement of paper money by US, UK and European governments and central banks. I did not choose this Theme because it's not "nuanced" and I didn't want to suggest that, to be a valid investment, every Theme has to be a grand slam home run.

Managing a downturn

Nothing lasts forever. Any Theme, like any individual investment, has a life cycle and will enter periods of cyclical decline or possibly secular (permanent) decline. For example, Gold and Silver was a very strong Theme for me from 2001 to 2012. After hitting historic highs (on a nominal and inflation adjusted basis) in early 2012 both gold and silver did poorly from late 2012 through the last quarter of 2015. Many analysts, including the writer, believe that over the longer haul, say the decade to come, gold and silver will be very successful investments again; the underlying Theme is the debasement of fiat money through very damaging central bank monetary policies.

Right now in the second quarter of 2016, gold and silver have strongly rallied and a case can be made on fundamental grounds, technical analysis grounds and socio-political grounds that the outlook for these two "precious metals" is very strong. The Theme's longer-term trend seems to have decisively reversed.

Against that positive reversal we have an interesting situation developing for Apple. After years of legendary growth and performance Apple's prospects have seemingly reversed. I-phone sales declined in the first quarter of 2016 and no new blockbuster product offerings are in sight. Recent offerings such as the watch and glasses have not produced market-moving results.

This does create a conundrum for the investor. Downturns in a Theme are unsettling and costly from a capital conservation perspective and the exposure has to be managed.

What is to be done? There are two sensible approaches:

1. Maintain a small position in the Theme, say 5–10% of your total portfolio (and if you believe, for example) in gold and silver as a major investment hedge it may be worth thinking about your exposure in terms of your total net worth, or "total portfolio"

2. Be flexible and opportunistic – this can be hard for non-professional investors. By this I mean, if you have sold out of a key Theme (one in which you continue to have a lot of "conviction") be prepared to buy back in even at a price higher than you sold out at, if you believe the Theme has re-entered an uptrend. This is emotionally difficult for many investors, but it has proven time and again to be a perfectly sensible and profitable strategy. Stripped of the emotion involved, it's easy to see, looking at the long-term price performance of individual stocks, market indices and Themes, that it has been demonstrably the right investment decision in many instances.

How to determine a re-entry / re-purchase point? Take a look at an investment's longer-term price chart, say 3 – 5 years. Once the price rises above a previous high and stays above it for several sessions, a week, a month – that is a good and legitimate re-entry point.

Maintaining a position in a Theme over the long term or re-entering a Theme from time to time as opportunities arise is not the same thing as "buy and hold no matter what!" or somehow being tied to repeating or being restricted to some limited universe of investment choices.

Themes should be based on convictions. If your reasonably non-emotive evaluation of that conviction leads you back to that Theme then you should pursue it, but do it in a "risk managed" way. Applying good and consistent Risk Management principles is the only tool we have to manage our judgments and convictions. An imperfect analogy: we're driving down a highway, the posted speed limit is 65 mph but it's raining very hard, it's dusk and visibility is worsening and there are "those other drivers". Risk Management tells us to slow down, no matter what the posted speed limit may be. We don't have to get off the highway if that remains the best way to get to our destination; we can just drive defensively and reduce our risk. Risk Management is the only real fail-safe we have, and we need to use it, accepting all the while that there are no guarantees and sure-fire solutions in 'the battle for investment survival'.

Chapter 3

Risk Management

I believe this is the most important chapter of the book – it is the most important process and discipline in investing. It's twice, three times as important if you, like me, are a retired investor aged 60 or above.

I've said it before and it's worth saying again: remember Graham and Buffet's Rules 1 and 2:

Rule 1: Don't Lose Money;

Rule 2: Remember Rule 1.

Most investors think of the stock market at a place to "make money". The sad truth is that for many, many private investors the market is really a place to lose money. Because the investor does not pay attention to capital conservation and risk management they lose money. They then exit the market disappointed and disillusioned. They then find themselves tempted back into the market, usually when a major rally is dying; they then lose more money and exit the market yet again.

I really believe that if you practice risk management one of the principal benefits of so doing is to avoid the whipsaw effect of being knocked out of markets and then re-entering them at inappropriate times and getting wacked yet again. Risk management enables to you avoid the big, unnecessary losses that erode your capital, your confidence and your long-term savings plan.

Defensive Investing consists of four key processes:

- Strategy development (self-evaluation, goal setting, investment style selections);
- Strategy implementation (portfolio construction / investment instrument selection);
- Risk Management (conservation of capital);
- Portfolio monitoring and management (strategy and goal review, strategy modification and portfolio rebalancing).

This chapter focuses on Risk Management techniques. Everything else we do right will come to naught (or worse) without rigorous and consistent Risk Management. I want to deal with Risk Management early on in this book because it is absolutely essential, and if for any reason, you can't agree with the concepts and mechanics set out in this chapter, then the rest of the book will not be a "complete" solution for your investment concerns. And much of your subsequent investment activities will only serve to increase the risk to your savings / your capital rather than help you meet your financial goals.

Risk Management is a bit like wearing a seatbelt and having a car with above-average safety features. These factors will not prevent accidents; they will, however, mitigate the damage you personally suffer and they are likely to save your life in most instances.

Yet again, we only have to remember our Rules 1 and 2 to know how important Risk Management is in winning 'the battle for investment survival'. See Appendix 3 for more discussion of Rule 1.

Several points should be noted now:

1 Risk Management is essential, but it's not difficult or complicated.

2 Risk Management can be done simply or we can add on "bells and whistles"; either way, it's critical and either way it will be effective in helping us to meet our investment goals.

3 Risk Management techniques are designed specifically to manage emotion in terms of our portfolio management. We will never fully overcome fear of loss, fear of loss of status and self-image, greed, hubris and all the other self-defeating emotions attendant with dealing with money and investments. But we can manage these dysfunctional emotions to mitigate their potential damage.

4 Risk Management is how we will conserve our capital. If only because of inflation, we need to grow our capital at a rate superior to the long-term rate of inflation. Capital growth goes hand-in-hand with Risk Management. However, the potential for loss due to poor or non-existent Risk Management is much, much greater on average than loss of value through inflation. Long-term inflation can average, say, 3% – that's not good. But the scope for repeated investment losses of anywhere from 20% to 25% ++ (a not uncommon range) is much more deleterious. See Appendix 4 for more on the effects of inflation.

The mechanics of Risk Management

I now want to review the principles and the mechanics of Risk Management. I want to stress the mechanics – the steps we can take to implement effective Risk Management.

But before getting into the core of Risk Management I want to briefly discuss an operative principle that governs the operating philosophy of Defensive Investing. That principle is often referred to as the "minimum effective dosage".

The minimum effective dosage in our context simply means that where possible we want to do the simplest, easiest things that are largely effective in meeting our goals. This is pragmatic:

- It recognizes that you don't want to spend all your spare time on your investments;
- You don't want to incur excessive costs; and
- You want a process simple enough that you will follow it regularly and consistently.

I said above that we can do simple Risk Management or we can add bells and whistles. This is equally true in terms of Theme identification and development, identification of access points for making specific investments and everything else we intend do. The added bells and whistles may well have an identifiable (quantifiable) beneficial effect but the problem is:

- The added benefit can be small if there is actually any added benefit at all;
- The bells and whistles can be complicated, laborious and possibly costly and the cost: benefit trade-off can be unattractive;
- The more complicated and drawn-out any process we undertake is, the less likely it is that we will do it consistently or rigorously; hence the complication factor becomes entirely self-defeating and should be avoided.

I will set out the simple Risk Management mechanics and I will suggest some bells and whistles but urge the Defensive Investor to keep the minimum effective dosage principle firmly in mind and do whatever it is (simple or complicated) that you will do consistently. Nothing else will work.

Age and Risk Management

There is a rule of thumb about age and Risk Management. The rule of thumb is to allocate your investments between higher risk assets (stocks) and lower risk assets (bonds) using your age as a sliding scale.

So, if you're 50 years old then you should have 50% of your portfolio in stocks and 50% in bonds. If you are 65 years old then you should have 35% of your portfolio in stocks and the remainder in bonds.

This rule of thumb is open to endless amounts of criticism. It is valid in that it takes into account the problem of time duration for making up capital losses. The older you get the less time you have and probably the less energy you have to claw back losses from the market.

It also takes into account the issue of declining competence to manage our investments actively as we age.

The problem with the rule is that it is really naïve to believe that in the present and future environment bonds are "safe". Not only are there credit risk problems with the issuers, but also there is now considerable interest rate risk (that is loss of capital if interest rates now rise, particularly due to inflation when you are holding low interest rate bonds, such as US Treasuries or UK Gilts).

But, if you need or want higher income than bonds can now provide, if you are interested in being an equity investor, then simple Risk Management principles and mechanics can greatly lower the risk of holding equities. Risk Management really alters the validity of this rule of thumb and suggests that you can take on and manage a lot more risk than proposed if you manage your risk with discipline.

Discipline 1: Money Management and diversification

The principal of Money Management is to limit your commitment to any one investment (and hence your total risk in that position) by placing a limit on the monetary value of the position, restricting it to a small percentage of your portfolio. Most fund managers do this and most investment fund charters limit the size of any single position the managers can take on behalf of the fund and its investors.

The corollary to limiting the size of individual positions is the principle of diversification. In trying to diversify the holdings in the portfolio you are trying to assemble a range of shares that are non-correlated or minimally correlated. Diversification is easy to describe but in practice very hard to genuinely achieve. The reason: the reality of our modern economies and markets is that of increasing correlation within asset classes (stocks or bonds, for example) and across both asset classes and geographic markets.

The correlation between the movement of the US and UK stock markets is so strongly positive you can't even achieve basic, effective diversification by investing across just these two geographically separate markets. See Appendix 5 for more on correlation and diversification.

To highlight how difficult and in a sense how "dynamic" the issue of correlation can be, a study done about three years ago in the UK found this "amazing" anomaly. The correlation between North Sea oil prices (Brent Crude) and the UK stock market oil and gas sector is just 0.29 (29%) but the correlation between the price movement of the oil and gas sector and the UK All Share Index is 0.73, almost three times greater – think about this for a minute. The price of an industry's principle product has less impact on the stock price movement of that sector than it does on a whole bunch of non-energy related but energy using / dependent businesses. There are good explanations for this particular anomaly but the important take-away for us as investors is:

- Real and effective relationships in the stock market are just not "obvious" or predictable by "common sense".
- Diversification is really harder than we may think it to be – in fact, so hard in the real world that we will want to simplify the process so as not to waste time and energy seeking a goal that is far too distant.

However, in contradiction to the above-mentioned findings it is very clear that the correlation between oil prices and energy sector stock prices over the last year has been very highly positive. The collapse in oil prices globally has ushered in collapse in major energy company share prices. Why this apparent anomaly with regard to the study? The only "obvious" explanation is the severity of the price drop in petroleum globally. The severity of drop changed investor perceptions and valuations of energy companies thus creating the strong correlation.

And to make things a bit more complicated: in order to achieve really effective diversification the laws of statistics say you need choose only 10 – 12 stocks; easy, except all the stocks have to have a very low co-efficient of correlation. Not so easy.

Every investor knows that during volatile market conditions (a phenomenon occurring with ever greater frequency and severity) the majority of stocks, whether they appear correlated or not, rise and fall together thus defeating the goal of achieving investment diversification. This is called "market risk or systemic risk and non-specific risk" in financial theory and differs from company-specific risk.

Company-specific risk can be diversified by building a portfolio of those 10–12 minimally or non-correlated stocks, e.g. generally speaking, stocks in different industries – even if your shares are correlated, diversification is still worthwhile because it can protect your portfolio from large-scale capital loss caused by company-specific problems with any one or two of your holdings.

Market-specific risk can only be diversified by investing across markets. That is, by investing in stocks plus fixed income plus real estate plus cash, plus precious metals, plus …

But … the degree of correlation among markets has increased as much as it has among equities only. This is presumably down to the better flow of information among investors thanks to things like the Internet and the fact that more and more investors are active in different investment markets simultaneously. Their behavior in one market is likely to be reflected in those other markets they are in, particularly when under stress.

We can find minimally or relatively lowly correlated stocks and asset classes by running basic statistical analyses for correlation of historical price movements. And, at least in theory, diversification of asset classes leads to higher returns with lower investment risk. But the reality is:

1 In practice, as cited above, the trend in investment markets has been for many years now towards greater correlation, not less.

2 Secondly, straining to achieve statistical diversification can simply lead us to stocks or alternative asset classes that aren't attractive in themselves or appropriate to our particular financial circumstances and investing skills, and which we may be unable or reluctant to access.

Minimizing risk

If we can't achieve real statistical diversification we can use simple Money Management to minimize the risk taken on every investment we make.

Typically, traders will limit each position they take, and each trade they make to no more than 5% of their total portfolio. In many instances, traders may limit individual positions to 2%

or 3%. The limit you place on each of your investments can be a function of:

a. Your overall risk tolerance. The more risk-averse you are, the smaller the limit should be.

b. Your perception of the risk of a particular investment. If you really feel, based on a reasonably objective analysis of the investment and the investment environment that the position is of lower than "average" risk, you could expand the limit to 7.5% or 10% for example.

   This kind of flexibility is good, but can be dangerous since it is so obviously open to abuse (and here we are talking about self-abuse!).

c. The number of positions you can have which you can effectively monitor.

   Investment funds can run the gamut from more than 50 different stocks held to 20 or fewer. It is very hard to monitor, manage and stay abreast of the developments of, say, 50 different stocks on your own. Unlike a large fund which may have two managers and several assistants / analysts, you are on your own and it is ineffective to over-burden yourself.

   If you are looking for guidelines I will venture the rule of thumb that 20–25 positions is really the sensible limit anyone alone can effectively manage.

   Within a portfolio of 20 or so positions you can include a range of very different investments constructed using the Core and Satellite process (which we'll deal with in Chapter 4). You can have practical diversification and you can have some concentration when you feel strongly about an investment opportunity.

This is how Money Management works. Let's say you have a portfolio of $100,000, you have 10 equal sized positions (you invested $10,000 in each of the stocks you bought) and you set a stop loss (say, on average across your holdings) of 10%. This means that in relation to any one stock you won't lose more than $1,000 or 1% of your total invested capital. We could increase the stop loss to, say, 20% for a particular stock and again we wouldn't be risking on that stock more than 2% ($2,000) of our capital.

As you can see, Money Management is a powerful Risk Management tool. It's also a potentially powerful profit management tool because it allows you / enables you to take some bigger risks with specific positions which you would view as being possibly exceptionally profitable without excessively exposing your total capital to greater risk than you would be normally comfortable with.

Money Management is critical because the individual risk of the stocks we own is very likely to vary widely, particularly if we use a Core and Satellite approach such that every stock we own isn't Johnson & Johnson (or Glaxo SmithKline) and its equivalents in terms of risk.

Money Management protects and conserves our capital. If you "want to bet the ranch", go to Las Vegas and have a good time, but don't do it in the stock market or with your core capital.

Let's sum up:

- Manage your per position exposure;
- Don't pile on more positions than you can reasonably monitor and manage.
- Your portfolio will consist of more than one investment and across your portfolio you can easily build a range of risk (just don't buy a portfolio of all oil exploration stocks, all "disruptive" tech stocks, etc.). A diversity of companies should provide, in itself, a strong, basic risk diversification.

> Going back to the issue of market risk, in the event of a "crash" your whole portfolio is likely to suffer. Yes, there have been days and weeks where losers outnumber winners by a big margin in downturns. Our saving grace here is not diversification, it's the use of stop losses on every position we hold.

Allied to the concept of Money Management there is another tool we can use which is based on a very simple concept. The most volatile stocks in your portfolio put you most a risk. If you have two stocks and one has an average historic volatility (up and down swings) of say 35% (not in the least uncommon) and the other has an historic volatility of say 10% which stock has the potential to inflict a bigger hit to your portfolio? Of course, it's the 35% volatility stock.

Based on this concept we can build a simple risk management tool.

- Check the historic volatility of the stocks in your portfolio
    - You can do this by simple looking at a 3–5 year price chart which will allow you to easily and visually determine price volatility
    - You can calculate the volatility by just picking say 24 or so monthly price points and comparing them
    - You can also subscribe to a website called "TradeStops" which calculates stock volatility using a proprietary algorithm.
    - You can simply use a stock's historic "Beta" (the ratio between the movement of a particular stock price and some relevant stock market index). The higher the Beta the more volatile the stock

When you have identified you high volatility stocks the risk management action is either jettison the position if you are not enthusiastic or committed to it or to simply minimize the position as a percentage of your total portfolio. In general high volatility stocks are the ones that will hurt you significantly in a downturn (they may also be the ones to most help you in an up-trending market). Because of this duality using "position sizing" allows us to retain a high volatility stock that we think has substantial capital appreciation possibility while still managing the downside risk to our portfolio. This is a very simple but genuinely effective risk management tool.

Discipline 1

A note on correlation

There are two simple ways of approximating the co-efficient of correlation in order to achieve higher levels of diversification:

- Firstly, look at the price charts for your stocks and overlay one stock on another on a chart and observe the price patterns over a time period. This will give you a very easily understood, visual representation of correlation (we'll deal with charts in Chapter 8).
- Secondly, you can always find the Betas for your investment from websites such as that of your broker or MSN Money, Yahoo Finance, Investors Chronicle (UK) and many others. Beta is a measure of the correlation / the movement of a stock relative to the market or some index of the market. A low Beta number means a stock is only weakly correlated with the market or the index.
    - Using the Beta number you can manage your market or systemic risk by using low Beta stocks or so-called "Smart Funds" with low Betas in your portfolio and you can make a simple comparison between two stocks or among several. If two stocks have similar market Betas (in a range of 0.80 - 0.87, for example) then they are going to be highly correlated between themselves while being relatively less correlated with the index they're being compared to.
- It's worth noting that two companies in the same industry (for example, oil exploration) are not necessarily "highly" or completely correlated because of differences in strategy, management, operating characteristics, etc. Will they be "significantly" correlated? Almost inevitably, but there are big differences between BP and Exxon, for example and from both a risk and growth perspective and this is worth keeping in mind.

Discipline 2: Stop losses

A stop loss is an instruction to your broker verbally or entered into the brokers' electronic trading platform by you to sell out a position at a designated level. It is also just a level you have in mind at which you will sell a stock.

There are essentially two types of stop losses. The first is a simple price designation. You have bought ATT at, say, $25 per share and you want to limit your possible loss to, say, $2 per share hence you enter a stop loss at $23 per share, or if possible, a so-called trailing stop loss of $2 per share (meaning if the stock rises in price the $2 stop trails it upwards).

If the $23 per share level is hit by the stock, your broker will sell it for you. He or his electronic trading platform will sell the share as soon as a price of $23 is made in the market, but he may not be able to get that price if the market or the individual share price is volatile and hence you may only get out of the position at, say, $22.85. (You can, by the way, give instructions to your broker not to affect the stop loss at a level below $23 if that price can't be achieved).

The second type of stop loss instruction, and the one I greatly favor, is the trailing stop loss. Not every electronic trading platform or broker can or will accept a trailing stop loss, but most major brokers in the US and the UK do.

A trailing stop loss is one where you designate either a monetary or percentage change in price which if hit will trigger the stop loss sale. The great thing about a trailing stop loss is that it trails the stock's price as the stock moves up and down, thus allowing you to lock in gains and without having to review and manually re-enter a stop on an internet trading platform or reinstruct your broker.

The trailing stop loss operates in the following manner. You buy ATT at $25 per share. You then enter a trailing stop of say, $2 or for example 10%. The initial trigger is usually the last price recorded by your broker's platform. So if ATT stock rises to, say, $30 and you have a 10% stop loss, if the stock then subsequently sinks to $27 your stop loss will be triggered, locking in a $2 per share profit on the position. If you entered a monetary trailing stop of $2, then if the stock rises to $30 and then subsequently falls to $28 your stop should be hit, preserving your $3 gain. To be clear, if the share price doesn't rise but falls by either 10% or $2, the stop will also be hit, thus limiting your loss.

The types of stops you can enter can usually be found and initiated on the drop-down menus of the trading page of your broker's Internet platform. Additionally, broker websites such as Fidelity Investments also have a link to trading terms definitions, so if you are unsure of the option to select you can follow the link to their dictionary function. If the website doesn't have a glossary, just use an Internet search to get a definition of any financial term.

Physical vs. mental stop losses

There are investors and analysts who are opposed to using automatic stop losses instead of mental stop losses. A mental stop loss is simply setting a price point where you want to limit your loss or take a profit. You have to act and act promptly and consistently (no fudging, no second-guessing yourself or the market). An automatic stop loss is as described above, one where you have entered the stop instruction into your broker's trading system and it will be executed without you doing anything further (you can always amend the stop, but don't do so without very good reason).

Using mental stops tends to be self-defeating due to emotionality. When the stop level is reached, the investor then finds 10 reasons why not to initiate a sale, almost all the reasons being governed by emotion rather than rational analysis.

There are investment advisors who do not advocate using stop losses but only selling out of any investment when you think the investment argument for the stock has changed because of economic, industry or company-specific reasons.

This sounds reasonable, but in the absence of a clear news flow about why and how things have changed, this is not so easy to determine. Between quarterly or half-yearly reporting dates for company performance, it can be very hard for the private, small investor to glean any useful information about changes in the company's performance.

Setting a stop loss

I strongly, strongly advocate using automatic stop losses. Sure, you can set stops that are too tight and hence likely to get hit as a stock moves within the trading range it has established over the last months or longer. (Your stop is hit and then of course the stock rebounds and you want to kill yourself from remorse). This trap can be avoided by looking at chart of a company's share price over, say, the last three or six months to determine the fluctuation range of its share price. You would then set your stop just outside that range if you were comfortable to do so.

Real Estate Credit Investment price performance chart

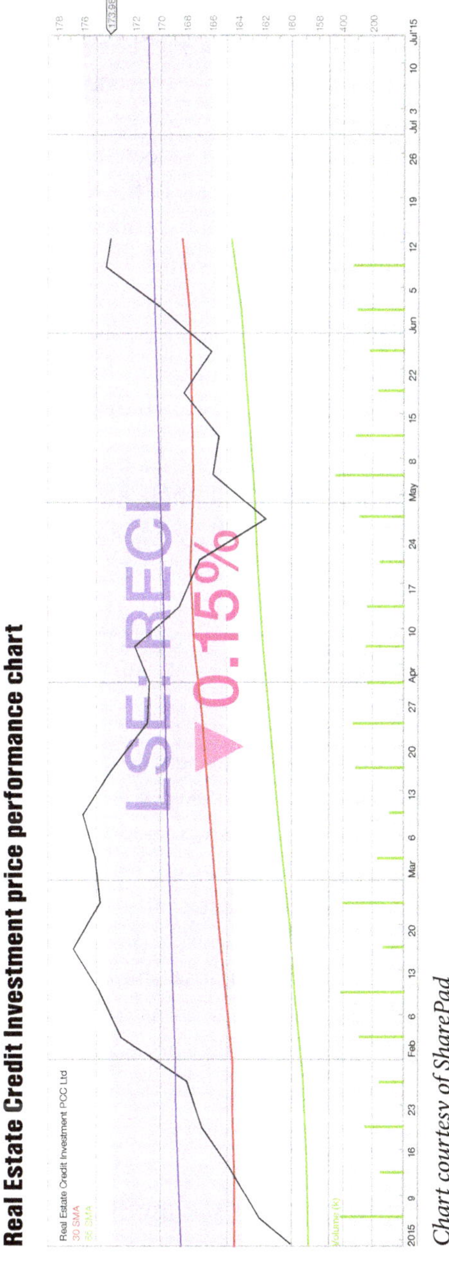

Chart courtesy of SharePad

Take a look at the chart above. It's a screen shot taken from a UK website call SharePad which I subscribe to. The chart is a 6-month price chart for the London listed real estate lender, Real Estate Credit Investment.

Using SharePad's functionality I simply selected from it options menu the drawing of a "price channel" of the last the 6 months of trading. The line running through the colored channel is RECI's closing prices, daily, over that period. The channel plots the share price volatility and in doing so gives you a sense of where you might set a stop.

You can see that the channel is pretty narrow, 166p–176p, only about 10% difference from bottom to top. The way to use this information is:

- Let's say you bought the shares at 166p around the beginning of May. You would want to set a stop loss (mental or automated) at around perhaps 156p. If RECI's price breaks below your stop and stays there for around a week to two weeks that is a reasonable signal that its price action has "broken down" and may well head lower.

- A second way of using the chart and setting a stop loss is, regardless of the price you purchased the shares at, you would probably want to set a stop at, at least, 10% and maybe around 12.5%–15% depending on your risk tolerance. You know from the chart that a 10% price fluctuation is "normal" for RECI based on its recent 6-month history. A breakdown in the share price of more than 10–15% should thus be seen as a big signal that something is wrong and the share price has a good chance of heading much lower.

You can use any other charting website you want, including BigCharts, Yahoo, Investors Chronicle, MoneyAM and so on. Just bring up a share price chart for the investment you are interested in, take a look at the price range over 3, 6 or 12 months (or longer if you want) and you will get a very good, very easily understandable graphic representation of where stop loss limits would be sensible given a particular investment's volatility.

Take a look at the BigCharts chart below for BP.

The trading range over 6 months has been approximately 470p on the downside to 500p on the upside. That is a trading range of about 6%. Clearly it would not be useful to then set a stop loss level of less than 6%. Something closer to 10% plus would be a good level for a company of BP's size and market liquidity.

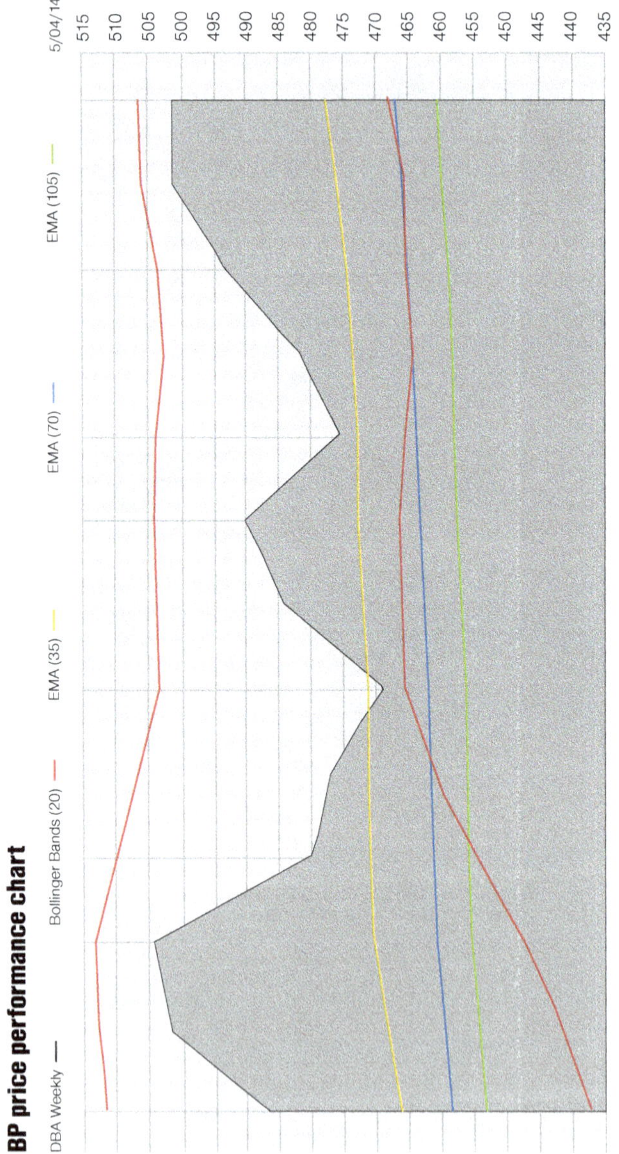

Chart courtesy of BigCharts

As already mentioned, some market professionals are opposed to automatic stop losses because they are published as selling prices on market information pages, the kind of in-depth information professional traders subscribe to, and as such your stop (along with many others) is known to traders who might want to act on it. The market information detailing offered selling prices for a stock (which would include your stop price) is vital information for a trader plotting a short sale and determining the possible profitability of the trade.

The above point is correct in terms of market practice; however, I'm personally very skeptical of this danger to the atomistic investor of using automated (non-emotional) stops. Why? Because our positions are so small. As I understand the practice, these sell orders we effectively create when setting a stop are ranked in time order of submission and are hit on a "first come / first serve" basis. This raises the question of how likely any one person's stop is likely to be hit unless there are very large buy orders placed at the price level your stop denotes.

For we small investors, I think, on average, and I do need to emphasize the "on average" qualifier, our stops are not unduly exposed. And if you are happy with the stop level you've set, then if it's hit, it's hit, and that's all that's worth bothering with.

I would also point out that when we are talking about positions in large, liquid stocks (S&P 500, FTSE 100 and 250 stocks) the ability of a professional trader to drive down the price of an otherwise well performing stock (and where there has been no event such as the BP's Macondo Gulf of Mexico oil spill) is very limited because of the amount of money and risk that would have to be applied to effect a downdraft of even 5% in the share price. This does happen, it's perfectly possible, but in normal market conditions it is a relatively rare event.

Advantages of automated stops

- I believe best practice and the minimum effective dosage is to place an automatic stop, place it a sensible level and avoid emotion. Emotion will almost always defeat you and sometimes take a large bite out of your capital. Market manipulation by professional traders may occasionally defeat you, but I suggest that the cost will be very limited compared to the toll extracted by emotion.
- Cutting your losses and letting your profits run is simply critical to long-term investment success.
- Automatic stop losses are designed to overcome the basic and profound investment behavioral problem of fearing losses, fearing the pain of losses, fearing the loss of self-confidence and self-worth, postponing critical decisions, self-delusion about the investment process, panic, remorse, irrationality and so on, and I can't repeat this too often.
- I'm not sure I know anyone, least of all myself, who can consistently use mental stop losses free of emotion.
- I do know of well-known, established traders and fund managers who have suffered grievous losses on positions because they didn't use stops, either automatic or mental, or could not execute mental stops. It is more painful to look back on something like a 50% loss on a position then to look back on having foregone a 10% profit.

The risk: reward trade-off

Traders often calculate / estimate the risk: reward trade-off for any trade and many traders would not enter a trade unless they thought the upside (the potential price appreciation) was at least two or three times their downside risk (which they would lock in via a stop loss).

As investors we can and should make a similar calculation, but with a view over a much longer timeframe than a short-term trader would use and allowing for more volatility (price fluctuation) than a typical short-term trader would accept.

I don't a have a rule of thumb for you, but it's perfectly sensible to use at least a 2: 1 reward to risk ratio for investments where you are focused on growth. In those situations where your primary focus or equal focus is income, you might want to consider a 1.5: 1 ratio as satisfactory and set a stop related to the income / dividend yield of the investment.

Support and resistance levels

A second way of setting stock specific stops and again using charts for the stock is not to look at the overall price fluctuation over the time period you choose but to look for what are called "support levels". These are price points over your chosen time period below which the stock has not fallen (or if it did fall below the support level, the fall was not deep and the price rebounded quickly).

Support levels are price points where investors stepped in to buy the stock and hence support its price because they felt there was value in the stock at those prices.

The corollary to support levels are "resistance levels". Resistance levels are prices at which investors start selling the stock because they no longer believe there is additional value or upside in the stock at that higher price.

Let's look at the chart below and determine a support level that could be the basis for setting a stop on this stock.

The stock is Annaly (NLY), the mortgage REIT (real estate investment trust). The chart provided courtesy of BigCharts, an excellent, free web-based stock charting service that you can easily access which provides a wide range of charts for US, UK and other international securities.

Looking at the chart, the bars show NLY's prices at the close of each week over the six months from November 2013 to May 2014. Look at the shortest bars, the second monthly set on the left side of the graph. This gives us an average low price for the period of about $9.60 to $10 per share. And you can see that the price was "supported" / recovered every time it bounced around this area. This is a measure of the support level. Buyers stepped in at this price range every time the stock sunk to this range. In the case of NLY, it is very fair (in hindsight) to say that the dividend yield on NLY, which was going toward 12% at that price range, was the reason buyers came back into the stock. 12% was a very attractive income return for the risk characteristics of NLY and the market-wide interest rates at the time.

Now, let's look at the most recent highs on the right side of the chart, May 2014. Here we can see the resistance level for the stock as it now stands, at around $11.50. On the day I did the screenshot of NLY, the current share price was $11.68+. The stock has at least temporarily broken through its resistance level and could go higher, or by the end of the trading day or within a day or two, it could just as well retreat right back to the resistance level of around $11.50 per share.

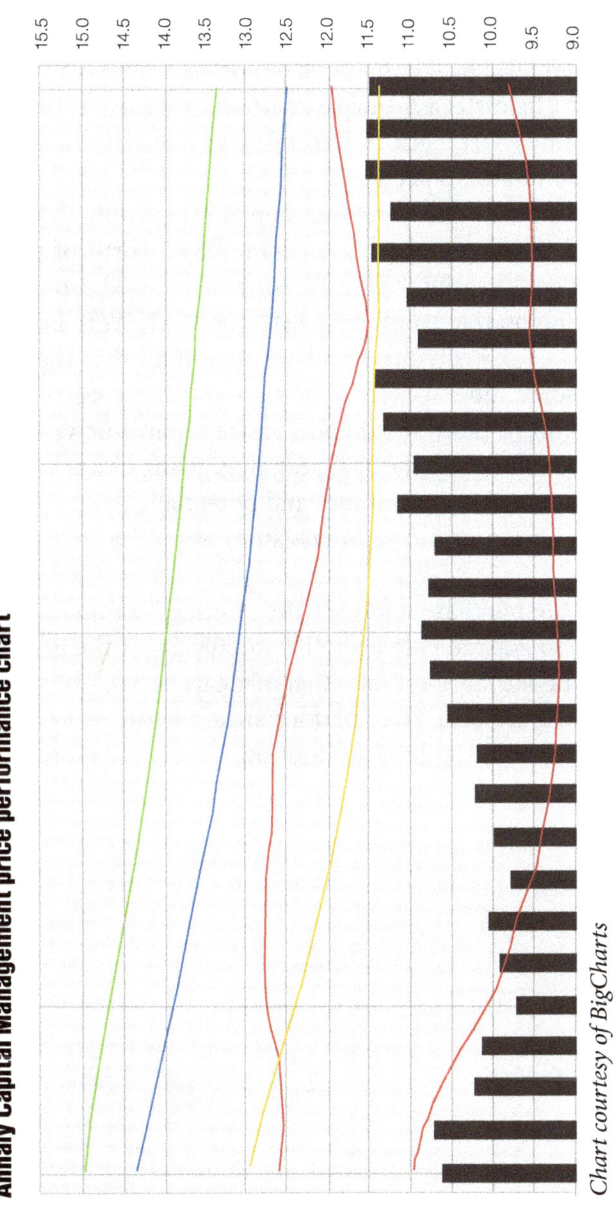

Annaly Capital Management price performance chart

Chart courtesy of BigCharts

Let's say we buy NLY for $11.68 per share; where are we going to set our stop? We've identified a short-term support level of around $11.50. We could also try to identify a longer-term support level by looking back 6 months or one year.

The chart below is a 6-month chart and we can see on the left side of the chart, back in December 2013 another support level of around $10.00 per share.

It would not be wise to set our stop at $11.50, only 18 cents or 1.5% below our purchase price. One day's worth of price movement could easily trigger our stop. If we used $10.00 as a stop loss point, that would be a 14% stop level. We're buying NLY for its 10.27% dividend and we also think that there is scope for some modest price appreciation (maybe 5% on the low end to much more should NLY move towards its 52-week high of around $15 over the next year, thus giving us a 15% total return at an estimated minimum and potentially much more) a stop around $10 or $10.50 (a 12% stop) would be eminently reasonable.

If, post the purchase and over the ensuing months, something were to happen either to NLY specifically or the market in general or with interest rates that made us nervous or skeptical about future NLY price performance, we can always and easily tighten the stop level to limit our potential loss to less than 14% or 12%.

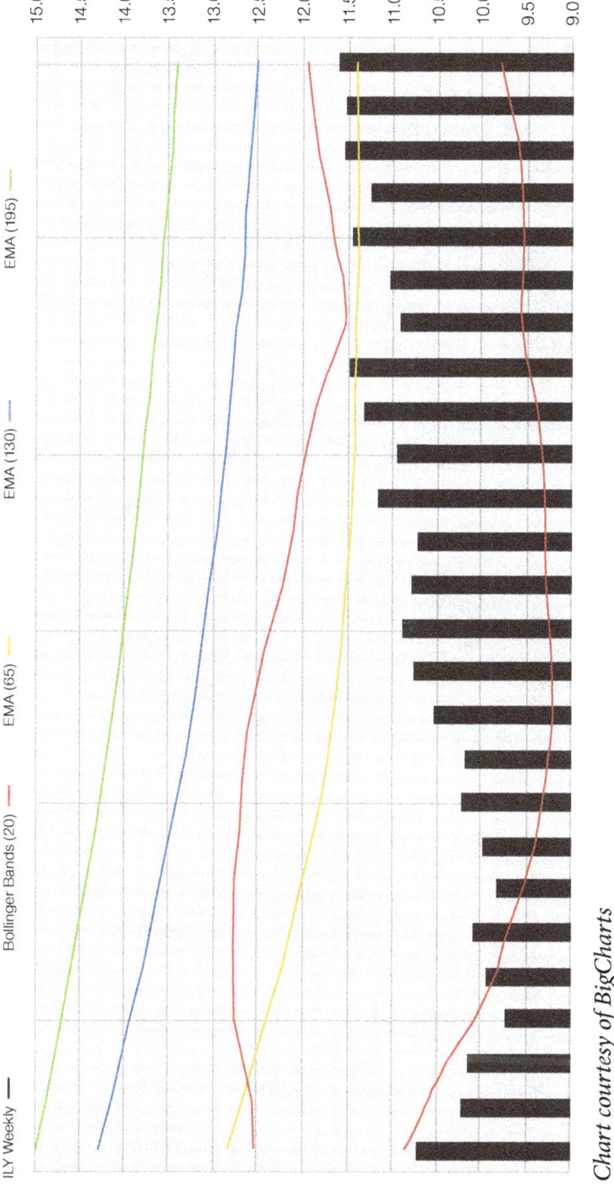

Chart courtesy of BigCharts

We're buying the stock well below its 52-week high of $15.25 but significantly above its 52-week low of $9.66. We have more potential upside should NLY regain or get very near that $15 figure than we have potential downside should NLY fall towards the low of $9.66. We have, with the 10% dividend included in our thinking, a good risk: reward ratio.

With regard to market or systemic risk, NLY has a market Beta of 0.19 (in effect 19%), meaning that if the market were to fall by 10% in value, NLY is estimated to fall by only 1.9% based on its market correlation over longish periods of time. Given the state of the world today, market risk is a much greater risk for us than NLY's company-specific risk, but even here we have some risk mitigation because of NLY's very low Beta (co-efficient of correlation with the US stock market).

Let's do a complete risk overview of our purchase of Annaly:

1 Let's assume we have a $100,000 portfolio and we buy $10,000 of NLY stock at $11.68 per share (856 shares) i.e. 10% of our portfolio, a relatively large proportion (a 5% position would be more conservative), but we're keen to get that dividend and we believe NLY is relatively low risk, because:

2 We believe the company is well run, it has a good track record, we can find lots of recommendations from mortgage REIT analysts, the company is well covered and well regarded.

3 Based on our research and reading we believe interest rates will not move up significantly over the next 12 months, hence interest rate risk is low.

4 Based on our research and reading we believe that while the market is heading from a crash again it's not likely to occur before mid to end 2015 and we're at early May 2014.

5 NLY has a very low Beta and this gives us cause to believe our downside risk is limited if the market turns down, by a little or a lot.

6 We're going to place an automated trailing stop of, say, 12%. (this means we are "stopping our loss" at $1.40 per share, 12% of $11.68)

7 With a 12% stop level and given the 10% portfolio exposure we have on this investment our probable worst loss will $1,400 (our stop loss) which is1.4% of our total capital.

8 We are planning to be in the stock for a whole year's worth of dividends and we will collect a 10.27% yield or around $1,027 on our purchase of 856 shares ($10,000) stock. We want the income and the income will cushion / mitigate any fall in the price of NLY over our holding period. We might not make our projected return, we might not make a 10% return, but we've got a 10% cushion.

9 The 52-week high is $15.25 – we have set a stop at 12% or $1.40 per share we will either:

   i. Possibly lose $1.40 per share ($11.68 - $10.27) or

   ii. Gain $15.25 - $11.68 ($3.57 per share) plus a potential dividend of $0.11 per share for a potential total return of $3.68

We now have a very good risk: reward ratio of 2.62x with our dividend or 2.55x without including the dividend (note: since we're buying NLY for the income there is no real logic in excluding the dividend from the calculation).

You can see that we can "play" with this risk: reward ratio by modifying our upside (remember by virtue of the stop loss we have "locked-in" our downside risk) to any level we think is sensible. Remember that in a fast moving, volatile market we might not get our stop effected at $1.40 or 12%, the loss could be somewhat greater but the size of our risk: reward ratio is such that we can absorb some extra downside without much concern.

We can also look at our potential downside in Beta terms. NLY has a .19 Beta, so if the stock market (we'll use the S&P 500 as the index comparator) were to fall by even 20% we would expect NLY to fall by only 3.8% or from $11.68 to $11.23. Our stop is set to click in at $10.27 ($11.68 minus 12%). If NLY's Beta going forward during our holding period stayed at around 19%, we have a pretty low-risk investment based on the factors we can quantify and we can test. As you can see, there's a big gap in our favor between the Beta based price movement and our stop loss level.

Now it is worth noting that if you were to calculate a "downside only Beta", meaning a Beta derived only using negative price movements you might well find that any stock's downside Beta is greater or lesser than the Beta calculated using both up and down price movements.

Our potential percentage gain / total return is anywhere from 10.27% (the dividend without any price appreciation) to an upper expected range of 31% if the 52-week high is regained and including our dividend.

I think it is fair to say that any return from 10.27% upwards is a credible, attractive return given the risk, and above all, given that we are buying NLY as an income stock.

Using Beta, market forecasts and probabilities; a simple but very subjective bell and whistle

Let's say that market "experts" (and I use the word "expert" reservedly) estimate that there is a 50% chance of a major market correction of 20% (and 20% is the market definition of a major setback / a bear market). This prediction is based on prevailing political-economic conditions.

Using NLY as an example, we've set our stop loss at 12%; if the historical Beta of 0.19 holds true for NLY, then for NLY to fall by 12% the market would first have to fall by around 60% (about three times NLY's 19% Beta.)

If we estimate or read that there is a 50% estimate for a major market decline of circa 20%, then in simple probability terms the market is therefore estimated to fall by 10% (50% of 20% - we apply the probability estimate to the potential outcome).

Doing this adjustment means our expected worst loss would around 1.9% (19% - the NLY Beta of the 10% market drop). This probability calculation gives us added confidence as to our stop loss point and our risk: reward trade-off estimate. You could also take the view that in light of this calculation, it would be reasonable to lower the stop loss percentage from 12% to 8% on the basis that even this number would be unlikely to be hit, but if the worst came to pass we could meaningfully lower our potential capital loss.

Warning!!! The exercise above only addresses the "systemic" / market risk aspect of investing in Annaly. The "problem" (or challenge) of investing for income in high yielding financial company shares is that these companies are very, very interest rate sensitive. If market interest rates (e.g. US Treasury bond or UK Gilt yields rise or are estimated by the market to be on the rise) the Beta based calculation in effect becomes less reliable. Rising interest rates are often accompanied by stable or even rising stock markets, but high yield income shares will deviate from the direction of the market dramatically.

In this instance it is the company-specific risk which matters and an estimate of the likelihood and size of any interest rate increases that are the key variables, not the overall movement of the market.

Too much information? Then keep it simple and go back to setting stop losses related to your risk tolerance, the size of your position and the price fluctuation range of the investment.

Total returns vs. absolute returns

I want to stress an important principle. I am a so-called "total return / absolute return" type investor. Including dividend income in my risk: return calculations is central to how I view my investment process and goals.

As a total return investor, I take current income into account when assessing and choosing investments and calculating my potential returns (or losses).

An absolute return investor is an investor who does not structure or measure his or her performance against an index. As many of you know, a standard criticism of the mutual fund / unit trust management industry is that so many funds and managers invest to only do as well or somewhat better than a benchmark index. This means that the manager has done his or her duty if the benchmark index is down over a year by 20%, but his or her fund is only down by 17%.

Absolute investors simply want a positive return regardless of the market outcome (not easily achieved, by the way). A recent study of UK Absolute Return funds over the last few, turbulent years revealed very poor and often negative annual performance, but nonetheless the concept and the "aspiration" are very valid. If your fund manager only aims to do as well as a particular index, you can save money by investing in an index fund or index ETF, both of which have lower management charges because they just "index" –they build a portfolio with the same stocks and same stock weightings as the composition of the index benchmarked.

Some additional points:

- Why have UK Absolute Return funds done poorly? There's no simple, obvious answer other than weak managers, poor stock picking, too much reliance on income stocks and value stocks that have not performed well over the last few years. There is no inherent reason for the under-performance
- Passive / Index Funds masquerading as Active Funds. Interestingly, a number of regulatory authorities in Europe are looking at funds listed in their markets (Sweden, for example) that advertise themselves as "active investors" but which, based on the composition of their portfolios and their performance records are clearly really passively managed index funds. Financial journalists in the UK are also on to this and have written frequently identifying suspect funds. The issue here is that investors should be given a clear picture of what they're buying into. And, if it is effectively an index fund then the fund fees should not be at levels charged by actively managed funds. Fees matter over time. A 1% per annum fee compounded over five or more years costs investors a meaningful portion of their potential return, and fees at this level and above should provide value in return

Setting stops: some considerations

Setting stops can be as simple or as complicated as you choose to make it. The most important thing is to have a stop, and again, I believe an automatic trailing stop is best.

In setting a simple percentage trailing stop I'm using a simplistic, but I think realistic and pragmatic parameter. I'm using a process that I believe, based on hard experience, works in terms of Risk Management that, as I've said, is a critical aspect of investing.

Using a percentage stop may seem naïve but setting a simple percentage stop loss is within everybody's competence. All it takes is being realistic about your risk tolerance level. Being realistic means not pretending to have a greater risk tolerance than you actually can manage and not setting stops so low (so tight) as to be unrealistic in a market context.

I can go beyond the minimum effective dosage and set my stops based on chart and price analysis. This is neither difficult nor particularly time-consuming and does improve the process to some greater or lesser degree.

Going back to the issue of setting stops with respect to dividend yields, I might not survive the whole annual dividend cycle for any stock and might get stopped-out of a stock without having collected a penny in cash dividends, but that is a basic investment risk I have accepted simply by being an investor. It's still better to have a stop loss.

With regard to dividends I will want to consider what the so-called ex-dividend dates for NLY are. The ex-dividend date is set by the company and you must be an owner of the stock on the day prior to the ex-dividend day in order to receive that dividend payment (usually made about a week to a month or so later). To be clear: on the ex-dividend date the stock trades without a right to receive the dividend – if you buy the stock on that date you will not get the dividend, the seller will.

If a stock does go through its apparent support level it may not stop on the downside until it reaches the next historical support level. With Annaly it just so happens that the \$9.60–\$10 support level is the level that held over the period examined in our example. So to find another lower support level necessarily takes us back to a time period that may be too far away to be meaningful in any current context.

Summary

1 Risk Management is about capital conservation.

2 Risk Management is critical.

3 Risk Management does not have to be complicated to be effective.

4 The more complicated we seek to make Risk Management, the sooner we will experience what economists call declining marginal utility. In other words, each additional complication will add less and less value and efficacy to what we are trying to do.

5 A reasonably diversified portfolio composed of a manageable number of investments will help to manage risk.

6 Using automatic stops will help us overcome many of the behavioral problems that defeat investors, both professional and amateur.

7 Knowing and using our risk tolerance level will give us the best available solution to setting our portfolio and stock-specific risk levels and stops.

8 We can systematically, rationally modify and improve our stock-specific risk levels using the simple, accessible techniques set out in this chapter.

Investment strategy, like economics, is a social science and does not incorporate so-called immutable laws such as chemistry or physics (in the light of quantum physics, perhaps physics is not as immutable as we were led to believe).

Investment professionals and academics are paid and in part win their reputations by trying to find rules and methods for greater certainty in investing. Sometimes they succeed in doing this, sometimes they don't. But often they produce findings that, while looking elegant, are great in theory but cumbersome or dubious in practice.

As investors we need to approach what we can call best practice in investment management but we need to find practical ways of employing investment principals without doing too much harm to the theory. That way we can stay on a track that helps us win 'the battle for investment survival'. The practical application of Risk Management techniques is designed to do exactly that.

Dividend investing

On the surface income investing seems pretty straightforward and it largely is. But, of course, there are all sorts of wrinkles, different strategies and different opportunities. Firstly, I want to recommend a website called Dividend.com to you. It is an excellent financial website. As with many such sites, some amount of information can be had for free, usually just by registering; more detailed and potentially very useful information is only available by paid subscription. Take a look at the site, it's very good and it can provide you with a useful tutorial on dividends and dividend investing. Dividend.com only covers US equities; in the UK, you can use Dividend Max, which has many of the same features.

A quick overview

A bit of a complication in dividend investing is that a company's share price generally declines post the payment of dividend by about the amount of the dividend. (This happens due to the presumption that the value per share of the company is now that less the cash its uses to pay the dividend).

Hence, in the short run, dividend investing can be a zero sum game. This doesn't always happen, but for higher dividend yielding stocks it's often the case. The common exception are companies which happen to pay dividends at around market average levels and even grow them over time, which are not seen primarily as income stocks but rather are valued and perform in line with investor expectations of revenue and profit growth, and hence the payment of a normal, quarterly dividend will not have the impact it has on a company or structured fund whose focus is higher yields for shareholders.

Whether you qualify to receive a dividend depends on when you buy the stock relative to its ex-dividend date, after which you will not receive the most recently announced dividend. Having bought the stock before the ex-dividend date you (or through your broker's name) must be on the company share register on the registration date, which is generally about three or so business days after the ex-dividend date. Then there is the payment date – the day when company actually disburses the dividend money.

A website such as Dividend.com provides information on key dates for a huge number of stocks; it also provides yield information and the dollar value of past and prospective dividends and has its own proprietary rating system assessing companies in terms of the quality and reliability of their dividends. It also has information about companies that pay monthly dividends.

There are lots of dividend capture strategies designed to allow the investor to invest just before the ex-dividend date and then sell at a point not long after when the sale price of the stock doesn't wipe out the value of the dividend received because of the phenomenon listed above. I am skeptical of the efficacy of most dividend capture strategies and generally don't bother with them. They sound great in principle but I rarely see them working in practice.

Chapter 4

Portfolio Construction and Analysis

Portfolios are constructed to implement our investment strategy. Our investment strategy is directed at achieving our specific financial and investment goals.

Our principal goal is to grow and conserve our capital, but we are doing this to achieve the paramount goal of financial security and independence.

We can set growth targets and reasonable targets for capital conservation (meaning, we can accept a limited amount of transitory, realized or unrealized losses while pursuing a growth strategy). Our ancillary goals can include generating a targeted level of current income or minimizing the risk undertaken by the portfolio. But, always, the aim of the portfolio and how we construct and compose it is to meet our paramount goal.

In the next chapter we'll discuss idea generation, the process we'll use to develop investment ideas. In terms of portfolio construction we're going to use the Core and Satellite structure for generating and then organizing our investment ideas.

This form of portfolio construction, organization and management is focused on and built around a core set of positions which reflect the key goals to be achieved. Around the Core we'll build a set of Satellite positions – sub-portfolios that still reflect and facilitate our key goals but which use alternative investment strategies and are aimed at providing us with asset type and stock-specific diversification and targets of opportunity.

At any time over our investment experience, we might have several Satellite sub-portfolios or we might, at an extreme, have none because of our views on the state of the market.

The other key process we will use in portfolio construction is Investment Capital Budgeting, a simple process where we consciously, rationally allocate capital to our Core and Satellite portfolios in order to meet our risk: reward parameters.

The macro portfolio

We can take and should take a larger view of what our investment portfolio consists of. We can usefully extend the concept to include all our significant financial and non-financial assets. The point of looking at this, our macro portfolio (our total net worth), is to achieve an overall, long-term risk: reward balance for our total finances.

I don't want this chapter to become an essay on personal financial management but … we have to view our equity investment portfolio in the wider context of our overall financial situation, hence the matter merits a brief excursion.

The ultimate goals we're trying to achieve through the growth and conservation of capital is to achieve:

- Financial security; and
- Financial independence.

Financial security: For our purposes this means achieving a financial state where you and your family are secure. Secured in terms of housing; cash income to maintain an acceptable standard of living; secured in terms of healthcare provision; you are debt-free or carry a low level of debt consisting principally if not exclusively of a mortgage and possibly education-related debt for your children. You are largely without "extra-ordinary" worries about your financial viability. You can provide for your children's education and you can provide for your retirement.

Financial independence: This represents a qualitative and quantitative step-up. It means being able to live the life you want to live, the way you want. Obviously, this is a relative and subjective statement and for most of us financial independence will be achieved without the mega-yacht, the Ferrari or the waterfront estate.

Memorably, in the film 'Wall Street', Gordon Gekko's definition of financial independence was being really "liquid", meaning having enough cash for the private jet. We'll stop well short of this.

Everyone will have their own, hopefully, appropriate and realistic definitions of financial security and financial independence.

To achieve that long-term risk: reward balance we will want to include in our macro portfolio our non-equity market / non-fixed income market key investments such as pensions, housing, life insurance and other assets such as art and collectibles.

Pensions

In terms of portfolio construction and management over time, we need to take into account the presence or absence and the projected adequacy or inadequacy of company or private pension arrangements. This will impact the issue of how much we need to save and our investment goals in terms of capital available at retirement and how we manage investment risk. Among many other commentators, I urge readers, wherever they live, to not presume the State will help them out. Do not assume there will not be a social benefits crisis in the West with concomitant reductions in social support across the board or "means-tested" benefits (reducing the benefits for better-off taxpayers).

Pensions are a complex matter and the tax treatment and regulations of pension contributions and pension withdrawals is an enormous political football. At an extreme, we have in the last 20 years seen instances where bankrupt governments have literally seized their citizens' private pensions, rolling the assets into state schemes in order to raise cash.

As you will know, pension assets have been stolen by their company sponsors (for example, Robert Maxwell in the UK). Company pension sponsors have gone bankrupt, leaving behind under-funded pension plans inadequate to service the scheduled pay-outs to plan members.

Pension plans are equity risk and fixed income risk assets – those, along with property, are their principal if entire investments. The viability of pension plans depends on market movements.

Increasingly so-called defined benefit (or final salary) pension plans are disappearing, replaced by defined contribution plans. Defined contribution plans mean you make scheduled contributions out of your pay check and what you eventually have as a pension pot / pension capital at and during retirement is dependent on the growth and performance of the investment markets and the investments chosen by your plan manager (often in an asset allocation you must nominate).

Having a corporate pension and social security / state pension entitlement is a great thing but … just don't naively depend on these income sources remaining secure and not being degraded by events beyond your control.

The pension problem

As many readers know there are scores and scores of under-funded public sector and private sector pension funds. Interestingly, these under-funded and most often under-performing funds are associated with major international corporations and very large public sector funds representing civil servants in major cities and states in the US and various government entities at the central and county level in the UK.

This is not a problem confined to smaller pension providers who can't access "quality management". As mentioned earlier a big, big worry for pension plan participants is the conversion of funds from defined benefit / final salary to defined contribution where you "pays your money and takes your chances" on the market. Huge shortfalls in defined contribution pension plans are going already becoming the next great socio-political crisis of the 21st century for the developed world.

Studies have shown consistently that too many people are not saving adequately for their retirement, particularly given greatly extended life expectancies in the Western world. Dependence on your defined contribution pension plan (exacerbated by the effect of even mild inflation) is a scenario for financial misery.

Right now in the UK there is a clear recognition that the artificially low interest rates (and now in other parts of Europe – negative interest rates) are creating a crisis for savers, particularly older and very risk averse savers and for pension funds who current bond investments are producing pitifully little income with the prospect of potential capital losses on their fixed income portfolios when interest rates inevitably rise.

Housing

As mentioned in another chapter, the history of house price appreciation is considerably less consistent and stellar than popularly believed. Our views on house price appreciation or depreciation is severely influenced by the psychological phenomenon called "recency" (the same is also true of our perception of weather patterns).

Recent events have a powerful influence on forming our beliefs about long-term patterns without reference to the facts and actual trends.

Having a mortgage free house at retirement is a great benefit if only because it provides you with a place to shelter (the original intent of "housing"). The fact that in recent decades housing has been used a form of wealth building for many and as a cash register for others are not practices supported by the long-term history of house prices.

Housing for many of us is our principal investment exposure to the real estate market and our principal asset in terms of value. As such, the relative size of that exposure to the rest of our portfolio needs to be kept in mind. While we can subdivide the real estate market into residential and commercial and further sub-divide it by type, the reality is that all real estate has a high degree of correlation, particularly within a geographic region or economic region. Hence, we have a significant and largely uncontrollable exposure to that asset class.

The housing market

Dependence on the housing market to bail you out in your retirement is another potential slippery slope. The housing markets in the developed world have gone through periods of incredible boom and then bust over the last three decades. The trends in residential prices in many boom markets such as London, New York and other select cities around the world mask a number of realities:

- As seen in both the US and the UK over the last decade, booms in key markets have not been matched in many secondary and tertiary markets.
- Real estate markets are notoriously "illiquid" and they are very sensitive to government meddling.
- When you are caught in a real estate market downturn it can be difficult to impossible to sell your house at an acceptable price or at any reasonable price for extended periods of time.
- We allow the short-term cyclicality of housing markets to bend our thinking on housing as an "investment" as opposed to necessary shelter in the first instance and as a financial speculation in the longer term.

Life insurance

Simply in terms of planning for your family's financial security or your retirement, if the policy has a surrender value you will want to factor in the value, terms and conditions and the presumed security of the policy. The quality of the insurer also determines the security of the death benefit.

Art and collectibles

If you collect art, stamps or coins, etc. of genuine quality and realistic appreciation potential, then you will take the value and eventual disposal of these assets into account in analyzing your portfolio. But note, lots of collectors delude themselves as to the value of their collection and caution is required. "General" rises in the value of collectible categories aren't really "general". The prices obtained by celebrated or fashionable painters, alive or dead, or the prices of rare stamps at auction do not impact or extend to all art or all stamps. Not by a mile! Just like a generalized, nationwide rise in existing home sales prices can mean little for the value of any particular house.

The point of including these other asset categories into your portfolio construction and analysis is to address a couple of decisional issues: risk and risk: reward, and meeting quantitative goals.

Risk and risk: reward

The assets set out above are often considered to be low risk, but they are not riskless, particularly if your pension is a defined contribution and not a defined benefit / final salary scheme. And even if your pension is a company or civil service provided final salary / defined benefit plan, the risk of the pension plan failing along with the company or city / county government sponsor (in the US) is not a trivial concern anymore. Every bankrupted city or county tries to reduce existing pension pay-outs as well as future pay-outs as part of its financial restructuring.

It's also worth noting that, increasingly, companies are selling their pension plans to independent management companies / insurance companies to get the liability off balance sheet and away from the company / plan sponsor's responsibility. The long-term fate of the plan now rests with an unrelated financial management company and not your former boss.

The US pension guarantee fund (and its UK counterpart) is inadequately funded for its prospective liabilities and, come what may, is unlikely to bail out failed plans without severely discounting benefits to plan members. At the time of writing in the UK we have the BHS pension mess unraveling with the likely outcome that the taxpayer through the UK pension bail-out fund will have to take on the liabilities of BHS's 11,000 pension plan participants and those plan members will take at least a 10% haircut on their benefits.

Housing prices can collapse and can bottom for long periods of time; individual owners have no meaningful influence on the price of their property in housing downturns marked by lots of repossessed property overhanging the market and limited mortgage availability.

Meeting quantitative goals

The estimated future value of these other key assets will be a major determinant of how much you need to grow your financial market invested capital. That will determine investment decisions, including asset selection, Risk Management decisions and where future flows of investable capital (savings) are actually deployed.

I've set out above some of the risks associated with these other key assets we may have. And we must not be complacent about the future values of these assets and the financial security they may provide for us but neither would it be useful to be unduly pessimistic about the future benefit of these assets.

It's mostly a matter of caution and realism over blind optimism and the "normalcy" and "recency" traps we can fall into.

Achieving the optimum risk: reward balance

An operating principle of portfolio construction simply stated is to achieve an "optimum" balance of risk and reward. The optimum balance (which is quantifiable and can be graphed – see Modern Portfolio Theory in Appendix 6) is that mix of assets that meets your growth goals while also being congruent with your risk tolerance level.

The optimum balance and the optimum portfolio are subjective matters. Nothing is optimum if it requires you to go beyond your comfort level (and also beyond your reasonable ability to manage risk, particularly in volatile market conditions).

I'm not suggesting that we should not try to grow and learn and in doing so, whether we're talking about investing or skiing, for example, achieve ever-higher levels of proficiency and hence, comfort, while also exceeding our previous performance limitations. But, there is a big difference between striving to grow and improve and living on the edge without the mindset or skills to safely stay there.

If you want to live on the edge, do it! That may be a great life style idea for hobbies but it's not a great tactic in 'the battle for investment survival'.

In order to operate effectively you need to operate within your comfort level. And let's note that "comfort level" does not equate to being without ambition or being fearful or slothful. It means being able to take decisions unburdened by fear, anxiety and post-decisional regret, among other negative behavioral factors.

This doesn't mean you will never experience a degree of fear, anxiety or post-decisional regret. But that is very different from being burdened, driven by fear and anxiety. Great traders and investors are not fearful – that doesn't mean they're "brave" or "macho", it means that they specifically avoid entrapping themselves in situations where they can't function rationally because of fear and anxiety. They don't "over-trade", they don't take excessive risks and they keep their eyes on the prize – conserving what they've grown.

In Chapter 3 on Risk Management we set out some of the principles and tools for estimating risk. The tools for estimating return are readily available but also come with the standard disclaimer that past performance is no guarantee of future performance (and they may not even be good predictors of future outcomes). Nonetheless, we have the ability to estimate performance and risk and this provides a good, solid and rational framework for portfolio construction and long-term management.

Core and Satellite portfolio construction

As stated we're going to use the Core and Satellite structure for constructing our portfolio. I want to start the discussion by setting out some of the critical parameters we will use in structuring the portfolio and determining the size of our Core position relative to our Satellite positions.

No investment decisions can take place in the proverbial "vacuum". Remember, investors have to live in and be keenly aware of the world around them. Against that background we can make sensible investment decisions.

There are a number of widely accepted and practiced investment strategies ranging from Growth to Value investing and the contrasting Top Down and Bottom Up approaches, which are examined further in Appendix 7. The reviewed performance of the many differing investment strategies done by academics and market analysts looking at strategy data over long periods of time has produced two significant pieces of information:

1. Over longer periods of time (circa 10–30 years) Value investing has produced the best returns particularly if measured on a risk: reward basis. Risk can be measured and assigned to any one investment or a strategy using a number of metrics (discussed in part in Chapter 3)

2. Not surprisingly, the other principle finding is that all of the principle strategies "have their day". No strategy works (produces positive or above market results) every year. Depending on market conditions and trends, some strategies will greatly outperform or underperform others for periods ranging from 1 to 5 years

What the findings suggest, I believe, is that the core theme of any long-term portfolio should have a clear bias towards value but, in constructing a portfolio, we should build around that core, "satellite" positions to take advantage of what we believe to be temporary market conditions and trends. This may sound like an intellectual "fudge" but I assure you it's not.

No single investment strategy consistently performs positively or outperforms some benchmark index. This is entirely consistent with the world as we know it and the fact that markets are not wholly rational or consistent themselves and are a product of the collective psychology of its participants (investors, market makers, analysts, etc.).

Core and satellite portfolio structure is a hedge against allowing your chosen investment style (your investment prejudice) to hurt you in the long run because you are "fighting the tape / fighting the trend" in the shorter term.

Some analysts and writers have suggested that the best performing strategy over time is a combination of Value and Momentum investing – I largely agree with this, but in practice this is a very opportunistic strategy that really is best implemented by creating a Value Core and a Satellite sub-portfolio of Momentum stocks.

What is Momentum Investing? Very simply it is buying those stocks with current upward momentum. It's based on the theory and the consistent observation that stocks moving *strongly* upward or downward will carry on in that direction because of "momentum" just as objects in physics have a "tendency" to keep moving in their present direction.

Value investors, such as Warren Buffet, have been "right "over the long run. But many fund managers who were strictly wedded to one investment style and would not countenance themselves or their subordinates diversifying away from that style inevitably "come to grief". This has happened in the last 15 years to notable investors such as Bill Miller of Legg Mason funds in the US and Tony Dye in the UK, whose 2008 obituary from the *Independent* newspaper is excerpted below.

> "Tony Dye was one of Britain's best known fund managers, becoming a household name in the late 1990s due to his controversial opinions about the outlook for global stock markets. At a time when markets were soaring, Dye insisted they were overvalued and on the verge of a crash – a view which put him at odds with most other investors at the time and earned him the nickname "Dr. Doom".
>
> As early as 1995, as the FTSE 100 was approaching 4,000 points, Dye began to make the case that markets were too expensive. At the time, he was the chief investment officer for Phillips & Drew, one of Britain's biggest asset management firms, and by 1996 he had begun to move large sums of clients' money out of equities and into cash.
>
> In the years that followed, however, stock markets continued to soar, driven by the technology boom. But Dye stuck to his guns, avoiding the high-growth, high-risk Internet stocks, maintaining large positions in cash, and consequently ensuring that Phillips & Drew's funds significantly underperformed their rivals. By 1999, the firm was ranked

> 66th out of 67 for performance amongst Britain's institutional fund managers, and was hemorrhaging clients – and in February the following year, just weeks after the FTSE had broken through 7,000 points for the first time, Dye was sacked.
>
> Days later, his prophesy finally came true. Markets collapsed, and settled into a three year slump, which saw more than 50 per cent wiped off the value of global stock markets.
>
> A year later, Dye went onto launch his own fund management boutique, Dye Asset Management, in partnership with the former Foreign & Colonial pension fund manager Ed Knox. The new firm's main offering was a hedge fund called Contra, which proved popular with investors, and amassed some $400m (£197m) of assets. However, by the time Dye stood down from his day-to-day management duties a few years ago, due to ill-health, the fund had dwindled to just $70m."

Dye just could not be flexible or pragmatic. He would not expand beyond value stocks and into growth and tech stocks. Ultimately he was right, but at great cost to his investors, his firm and himself. We need to be pragmatic and that means not being rigid about strategy. Core and Satellite is a great tool for reasonable experimentation and learning and it helps us to reconcile the seeming "moral" issue of how to maintain a core belief while taking advantage of market trends.

There is a conundrum here. Let's go back to the tech and Internet bubble of the late '90's. You are a value investor, you are financially responsible and you are rational. You look at the Internet stock bubble, new companies without profits, without a meaningful business model suddenly valued in the hundreds of millions of dollars. You think this is "crazy" and you are right. But these stocks are soaring. What do you do?

You recognize the risk inherent in the "bubble". You recognize that you could exploit this and you could do so while protecting yourself through Risk Management. You don't have to think *you're smarter than everyone else,* you're not, but you do have a process for taking advantage of the "momentum", whether it's rational or not through the use of all the Risk Management tools we've delineated.

Taking advantage of these types of either bubbles or legitimate but transitory trends in a "satellite portfolio" is good risk: reward and it the best way to be "flexible" and opportunistic without being foolish.

The last point I want to make on this is that Warren Buffet, a truly great value investor, doesn't always practice what he ostensibly preaches (virtually no-one does and hence not itself meant to be a criticism of Buffet). Buffet has used derivatives extensively, despite having characterized them as "weapons of mass financial destruction" (which to a large degree they are and will be one day). The point here is that being opportunistic, exploiting market trends, diversifying styles and strategies around a core belief is wholly legitimate.

Changing views when facts change (as per John Maynard Keynes) is only reasonable and sensible. Being flexible is part of winning 'the battle for investment survival'. The late Martin Zweig, an outstanding American investor said in his book 'Winning on Wall Street':

> "I can't emphasize enough the importance of staying with the trend in the market, being in gear with the tape, and not fighting the major movements. Fighting the tape is an invitation to disaster."

(In the early days of Wall Street, traders received updates by a machine that printed out prices on a roll of ticker tape. Even today, with the ticker tape machines long gone, traders still call market action "the tape".)

Traders operate in a more volatile and much shorter-term environment than long-term investors. Successful traders practice rigorous Risk Management, one key feature of which is Money Management. We've discussed Money Management in Chapter 3 it is a basic Risk Management tool and carries with it lots of rules of thumb.

Money Management is about limiting position sizes to limit your potential losses. Limiting our position sizes is also critical to successful investing but we, as longer-term investors, can be more liberal in applying the actual metrics of managing position sizes than traders.

It is a standard feature of the investment charters of many mutual funds or unit trusts to formally limit the size of any one position the fund managers can take in order to avoid over-concentration of risk. Typically, position limits for any one stock may be set at, say, 5% of the total value of the portfolio. This can be extended to limit sizes for industrial sectors or geographic limits, particularly for so-called "Global Funds".

As many readers will know there is also a minority view. Just as in the cult American film 'Repo Man' (men who repossess automobiles) where the protagonist played by Harry Dean Stanton proclaims that "ordinary people try avoid confrontation – repo men seek it!" there are investors and funds that seek concentration of investment risk and reward. George Soros is probably the most notable example. This investment style is also somewhat euphemistically also called "conviction investing". Meaning, if you are risk tolerant and feel strongly about the reward potential for a particular stock, you will establish very large relative positions. See Appendix 2 for more on conviction investing. Soros is famous for criticizing a young associate who was concerned about the size of a position he had that was in the millions of dollars. Soros, when consulted by the associate, is reputed to have said "you call that a position!"

Diversification and position sizing

As mentioned, with regard to the concept and practice of investment diversification, a well-diversified portfolio can consist of as few as 10 to 12 non-correlated or minimally correlated shares. This suggests that it would be reasonable to restrict our position sizes to something around 8–12% of our total portfolio or for any one stock within a sub-portfolio.

It might be convenient to apply the above suggested metrics strictly but we can and should also use judgment by varying our position sizes around this example of an 8–12% range based on our own estimation of the risk: reward trade-off of each position and our overall view of the direction of the stock market.

While position sizes restricted to, say, 5% can be very effective in limiting risk, there is a corollary issue. How many individual stock positions can we effectively track and manage? Some practitioners will say that more than 12 to 15 positions cannot be managed by an individual investor. The use of stop losses can make managing more positions considerably less risky but not necessarily more rewarding.

We also have to keep in mind that when constructing Core and Satellite portfolios that we will want to set position limits for each sub-portfolio and then for each position within that sub-portfolio.

This process may seem more time-consuming than it actually is. Setting and renewing stops, and devising and implementing position limits are only done occasionally and, as such, need some concentrated time, but not much time in terms of ongoing time commitments.

It's also very important to note the following phenomenon. Let's say our portfolio size is $100,000. Let's posit that we have a position equal to, say, 5% of the portfolio (hence $5,000 in value). We set our stop loss in this instance at, say, 15%. This means that our maximum loss should not exceed $750 (15% of

$5,000). Our possible maximum money loss is 0.75% (3/4ths of 1%) of our total portfolio.

- Good Money Management principles advocate that we should limit any one position loss to somewhere around 1–2.5% of our portfolio value (in our example this mean losses of $1,000 –$2,500). The point of this rule of thumb is that a 1% loss, incurred on average, means we have to make around 100 bad investments before we're good and broke. This kind of thing should be very unlikely for a sensible investor capable of reflecting on his experience.
- Whether you want to tolerate 1% loss limits or 2.5% limits depends on your goals, your risk tolerance and your other assets.
- Taking steps to limit individual losses within the portfolio of our example of 3/4th of 1% may be sub-optimal – our positions may then be too many and the positive potential impact of a successful position may actually be too little to benefit the total portfolio. We'll spend too much time selecting, risk-managing and monitoring too many positions. What this aspect of investing mechanics does suggest is that taking bigger, conviction-type positions can be risk managed just by making reasonable changes in money management and stop loss parameters.

Final word: use your own risk: reward judgment but keep your positions within a 5–12% range; at the 12% mark we're starting to talk about conviction. Always use stop losses.

The Core Position

This is our "conviction position". It's the investment Themes we feel most strongly about in terms of providing us with the best risk: reward trade-off. This sub-portfolio may be an industry or sector Theme such as natural resources or energy. Or it can be a sub-portfolio built by implementing a specific investment strategy such as Growth, Income and Growth, Value, etc. This sub-portfolio will be our largest and the individual positions in it may be among the largest we take.

Our convictions can change over time as the "facts change", but if we see the need to hedge our conviction or explore other opportunities or strategies we'll do so through our Satellite positions. Meaning, we don't casually alter our Core Position. If we think we're right on our Core Position, we need to then give the Theme reasonable time to be realized. We would want to see either our stop losses hit to alter our positions or objective information showing that the facts underlying this theme and / or any one position had changed.

If we feel the need to continually and frequently alter our Core Position, we then need to reflect on and analyze what the problem is, what's causing us to do this? If the problem is we lack conviction, for any number of reasons, then the fallback solution is simply to make an overall change. Change the Theme to something you do have conviction in. And you don't want to rush to do this. A good fallback position is to focus the Core on Value Investment (if that is not already a theme) or income investing. As previously stated, academic and market practitioner studies have shown Value Investing as the best long-term investment style / strategy. With income investing, you at least have the benefit of accruing current income (dividends) so that your capital is not "sterilized" or "immobilized", and hence not working for you.

Our Core Position serving as our conviction portfolio should be on the order of 35% - 50% of our total portfolio. This is admittedly a big range, but the size depends on the investor. Not just their convictions, but also their risk tolerance, their ability to manage multiple positions, their comfort levels with alternative strategies and themes and transitory market conditions and socio-economic, political-economic events and trends that will impact the position size.

Within our Core Position we will want to set position limits. In terms of diversification, it will not surprise anyone to hear that within a Theme, within an investment style, within a market sector or industry, virtually every stock is going to have a high degree of correlation with its peers. Attaining real diversification is accomplished through the selection and construction of your Satellite sub-portfolios.

An example of Core and Satellite construction

Here's a straightforward example of Core and Satellite construction. Let's say your Core Position is Energy – a very strong, longer-term Theme for lots of obvious reasons. We can actually diversify within the Theme by ranging widely within the industry and selecting companies operating predominantly in different sectors. We can easily construct a Core portfolio consisting of:

1 The major integrated energy companies, e.g. Exxon, Chevron, Marathon, BP, Total, *et al.*

2 Exploration companies, e.g. Apache, Cairn, Anadarko, *et al.*

3 Nuclear energy (uranium, uranium miners and support services (e.g. Carrs in the UK which has a nuclear services division).

4 Energy service companies, e.g. Schlumberger, Haliburton, John Woods, *et al.*

5 Refiners –e.g. Valero in the US.

6 Natural gas explorers, producers or pipeline companies.

7 Alternative energy – solar, wind, biofuels, *etc.*

By diversifying within the industry or Theme we can manage individual stock risk. While all of these sub-sectors may move in the same direction at certain times, very importantly, they don't often move to the same degree, and this phenomenon helps mitigate our risk and any downside impact on our portfolio. Our real risk mitigation tool will always, however, be our use of stop losses.

It is worth noting that in a broad sector such as energy there are sub-sectors that play in opposition to each other. For example when petroleum prices rise alternative energy stocks tend to rise because the extra cost of production of alternative energy is mitigated by expensive carbon energy prices.

A Core and Satellite Portfolio

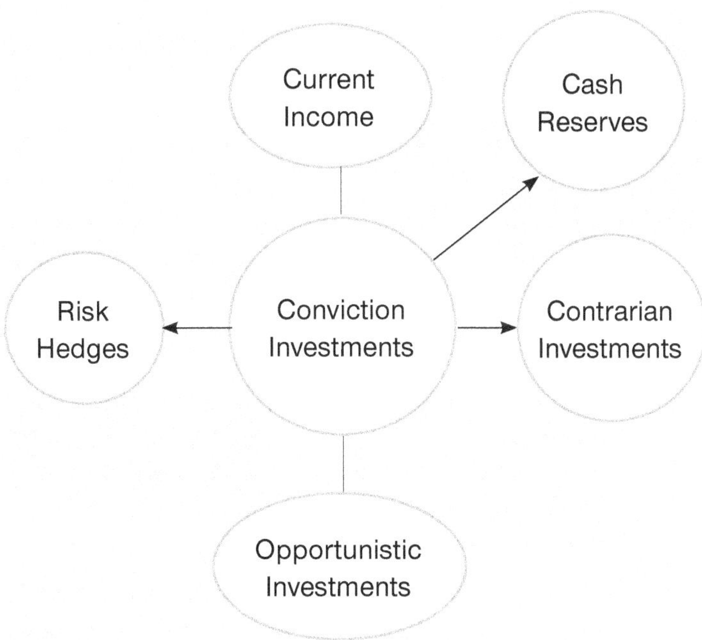

Satellite Positions

The nature and number of our Satellite sub-portfolios will depend on individual investor characteristics and market and economic conditions and trends.

If our Core portfolio accounted for 50% of our total market portfolio size, then we might have anywhere from two to five Satellite portfolios.

Our Satellite Positions can be opportunistic, or they can be built using alternative investment styles. They may focus on another theme or an industry sector. Again, we want to stick with some basic principles:

- Diversification: beyond opportunism, our Satellite portfolios should provide us with a degree of diversification related to our Core portfolio.
- We want to avoid having more Satellite portfolios or positions then we can effectively monitor and manage.
- Within any Satellite portfolio we want to have position limits.
- We may be intrigued to experiment with alternative investment styles, but we have to use discretion and common sense. In a low to non-growth economic scenario, for example, it may be very challenging to build a growth-style portfolio. It can be done; there will always be a handful of genuine growth stocks, but it will require a lot of stock picking. If it's not clear where the fundamental, real world economy is headed, then a growth-oriented portfolio could be a good potential hedge and a good contrarian opportunity
- We may want some of our Satellite portfolios or positions to be hedges against our Core portfolio, our other specific Satellite portfolios, or hedges against potential economic or political events and trends.

I want my Satellite portfolios to serve several investing functions.

1 I want to explore alternative investment styles to my personal core value orientation. Partly because it can be interesting, fun, enlightening and a way of growing capital. No one investment style is consistently successful year on year. Hence, exploring alternative styles is opportunistic, it's a hedge and it's a form of diversification.

2 I often want my Satellite positions to be in opposition to my investment beliefs because I know how much I don't know and I know how my prejudices can severely limit my investment success. I want to listen to the reasoned arguments of other investors, and where I think there's merit, I want to overcome my prejudices and take what I believe to be a sensible position (sensible in terms of risk limitation).

3 I use Satellites to hedge risk. I will invest in so-called "inverse ETFs" (see below) to hedge my positions in conviction investments such as gold, silver and energy, particularly when those investments are down trending in the short term. I also try to hedge the possibility of market downturns, particularly severe ones (e.g. a 10% ++ downturn in the key indices) or to hedge what I think are weaknesses in the real economy which will eventually be reflected in the stock market.

4 I use Satellites to build opportunistic positions. Investments in companies that are displaying so-called "break-out" price patterns. These tend to be short-term trades more than investments, but I use small position sizes and I am prepared to accept the consequences of taking losses, albeit limited thanks to my stops.

In order to limit the negative impact of my own investment prejudices what I often do is to look for a Fund, Investment Trust or an ETF that discloses positions in stocks I don't want to invest in directly. I feel much more comfortable leaving the management of positions that could have merit but which make me uncomfortable in the hands of a manager with expertise in that industry. Some personal examples: Biotech, I like biotech as a theme but I can't sensibly differentiate one company from another. Another example would be companies providing outsourced business services. I recommend this tactic to you. It is the easiest and I think most effective (minimum effective dosage) method for overcoming "closed-mindedness".

Hedging risk

The principal way we can hedge our investment risk is through the use of stop losses. We can also hedge by short-selling (or "shorting") stocks or using so-called inverse ETFs. Shorting (selling stock you do not own with the prospect of buying it back to close your trade at a lower price than you sold it for, thus crystallizing a profit) or investing in inverse ETFs can be used to generate profits when you believe the market or market segments are trending down; alternatively both processes can be used as genuine hedges (loss mitigants).

(Inverse ETFs and ETFs in general are discussed in Chapter 7, and using ETFs as hedges is discussed in Appendix 9.)

There is nothing wrong with building a satellite portfolio of short positions for profit. But it's very helpful to be clear about what it is you are doing, the logic and the risks and potential rewards for so doing.

The Core and Satellite construction discussed here serves lots of useful purposes:

- It is in effect the simplest way of dealing with the complexity of investment decision-making and management;

- It provides diversification;
- It admits of opportunity; and
- It gives us the ability to go beyond our own prejudices and comfort zones while the all the time maintaining strong Risk Management processes.

I mentioned that no one investment style is always effective. While I continue to maintain a long-term preference for value and income stocks, it's clear that opportunity almost always exists to exploit the market, go with trend, etc. I don't want to overlook an admittedly speculative opportunity that could usefully grow my capital by a few percentage points.

The sensible way to do this is to build a Satellite sub-portfolio that could amount to, say, no more than 5% or 10% or your total investment assets. Every position in that portfolio will be underpinned by stops, and since this satellite portfolio is purely speculative, I will use tighter stops, on the order of 5–8% plus, depending on the stock in question and views about the risk or volatility of that stock.

A model portfolio

As an example of what a total Core and Satellite portfolio could look like, I've set out below a model portfolio that reflects my demographics, my views and preferences. It is only a "model" in the structural sense, not in terms of its composition.

Core Portfolio: Allocation = 50%

Composition: Value and income producing stocks

Satellites: Allocation = 50%

1 High yield: Sub-allocation = 50% (25% of the total portfolio size)– companies and investment vehicles generating dividend yields above say 6%

2 Speculative: Sub-allocation = 25% – growth companies and potential short-term price break-outs

3 Growth companies: Sub-allocation = 25% – quality companies in major growth industries (such as biotech, telecoms, some aspects of the Internet) with long-term growth characteristics

How did I arrive at the allocation levels? The process is very simple and very straightforward; it's Investment Capital Budgeting. Let's review it.

Investment Capital Budgeting

In order to achieve the investment goals we set for ourselves, we evolve an investment strategy or set of strategies we want to employ. Our investment principles will lead us to a set of selected investments based on our understanding of the risk inherent both in our investment selections and the market as a whole, the potential returns from our individual investments and the overall direction of the equity market.

I want to emphasize the importance following / executing this "top down" process. If you don't start the portfolio construction effort by clarifying you investment goals you are going to end up with a random selection of investments that generally will not be suited to getting to your goal.

Many financial magazines invite readers to submit their extant portfolios to review by "industry experts" and their own journalists. What you will most often see in terms of the professional critique is simply that the investor having stated their goal is then inevitably shown to have just not picked a logical group of stocks that are congruent with the achievement of the goal.

We need to develop a view on the potential return on our selected investments; we need to quantify the possible returns and we want to think about the total return (capital appreciation and any dividend income). We will develop our views from researching our selections – what do analysts say? Do we think their judgments are sound and supported by the likely direction of the market?

In doing our Investment Capital Budgeting, we are simply going to allocate our capital to our Core and Satellite portfolios and then "sub-allocate" those allocations to individual positions. We will do this in order to meet our risk: reward goals.

It's easy to start the budgeting process by setting a portfolio-wide return goal. For the upcoming year and with respect to the outlook for the market and how that outlook could be impacted by events, we could set a return goal of, say, 15%. We want our total capital, our total portfolio value to increase by 15%, from, say, $100,000 to $115,000. (Please note, that a 15% return consistently over say 5 years would make you a star investor).

The only realistic way this is going to come to pass is if we so allocate our investments such that the "weighted" average projected return of all our positions equals at least 15%. If we happen to construct a portfolio where the objective weighted average projected return of our selections equals 10%, then reaching that 15% goal is on the one hand unrealistic / improbable, and on the other hand a matter of "dumb luck" were it to happen.

(And as many investment advice articles will tell you be very careful about the "dumb luck factor", it happens all the time when an investor, private or professional, has a run of "beginner's luck" by starting out in the early stages or middle stage of a long term bull market. The "buoying effect" makes the investor or investment manager think they have talents they really don't have. As Warren Buffet has said with regard to the onset of bear markets "when the tide goes out we see who's been swimming without a bathing suit").

In terms of total return, the good news is: if on average our selections had a prospective dividend yield (and estimates for dividend yields are very accurate because of the nature of company dividend policies) of, say, 3%, then in terms of capital appreciation we then need to try to achieve "only" 12% to make our 15% total return goal. (As already mentioned an annual return of around 12% on a consistent basis would put an investor in the superstar class. In any one year it might represent a real "home run", or it could be a very third rate performance in a market where the principal indices rise by, say, 25%).

Now that we have a reward goal we can start making portfolio level allocations and individual stock sub-allocations designed to meet our return goal. Having done that, we have to review the portfolio using our Risk Management tools to determine if we are comfortable with the level of risk, however we want to measure it, that our portfolios come with. It now might be necessary to go back and make changes to either or both allocations levels or individual stock choices to get to the risk: reward position we're happy with.

We might find that we can't achieve our return target with an acceptable level of risk and that target has to be re-set so we can operate along that "efficient frontier" particular to each of us where we are comfortable with the risks undertaken for the likely reward we may get.

This isn't difficult to do, nor is it very time-consuming given that you will only do this about four times a year reviewing and rebalancing at the start of each quarter or if there is a substantial change in the market and the composition of your portfolio as a result of stop losses being executed.

Core and Satellite portfolio construction using Investment Capital Budgeting

Below is another example of how we could construct a Core and Satellite portfolio and how to do Investment Capital Budgeting.

To start with, I'll set an income target that I want to achieve so that I can live off my income and not erode my capital or use as little of my investment capital as practical to maintain the life I want in retirement. If not retired then I might target an income number to bring my "total annual income" up to some desired level.

To meet that target every year I need to invest a set amount of my investment capital in a diversified portfolio of income producing companies and vehicles. I know from analyst research what the projected dividend yields for these investments are likely to be. (Websites such as Divedend.com serve this purpose very handily).

I want diversification and, depending upon the political-economic outlook, I will favor certain types of investments over others. Knowing the projected yields of that population of investments I'm willing to make allows me to allocate the amount of capital I need to invest in those securities to earn my income target.

In terms of my income target I have divided my investments between my Core portfolio and the High Yield Satellite portfolio. I will not meet my income target solely from my Core portfolio with only a 50% allocation of capital. That is one reason why I will also construct the High Yield Satellite portfolio.

The Core portfolio won't satisfy my income target because it is largely composed very good companies but with yields in the 4.5–5% range. I need to augment this portfolio through my High Yield Satellite portfolio.

I know that my High Yield positions are riskier and they are more volatile. I may not be able to maintain these positions over a full investment year, collecting all the dividends paid. My stops may get hit. I set my stops at levels less than the prospective full year dividend yield because these are not growth stocks and as income stocks unless market interest rates drop they are likely to have very limited price appreciation potential. And they're not necessarily value stocks in the strictest definition of the term. I'm not prepared to take capital losses in excess or much in excess of the prospective dividend.

After allocating capital to meet my prime target and my conviction (value and quality income) the remaining allocations are opportunistic. The growth stock position is composed of good companies with good growth prospects, but for me this is opportunistic because it is at variance with my core investment belief at this time in my life and given my financial status.

The important thing to remember is that these processes of portfolio construction and capital budgeting are tools with the purpose of insuring that we invest logically, non-emotionally and in a way that is consistent with meeting our goals. The number of investors who end up with portfolios that simply can never meet goals they are perfectly capable of enunciating is, as already mentioned, legion. The way around this problem is to use tools and processes that simply force us to be logical and realistic.

A theoretical portfolio

- Total capital invested $100,000 (totally arbitrary number for illustrative purposes)
- Income target for the year: $5,000 (5.0% yield on the total invested capital)
- Total return target for the year: 15% (yield plus capital appreciation of 10%)

Core portfolio: $50,000 (50% of total capital invested) – stocks: all income producing companies or funds:

- With dividend yields ranging 4.0–6.5%
- Number of stocks = 5 (20% exposure to each stock / $10,000 per stock)

- Average weighted yield of portfolio based on 5 specific stock choices = 5.0%
- Income = $2,500
- Potential capital appreciation = 5%
- Projected total return = Yield of 5% + capital appreciation of 5% = 10% of $50,000 = $5,000

Satellite portfolio – High Yield: $20,000 (20% of total capital invested) – fund and special purpose vehicles such as mortgage REITs, oil and gas production and pipeline royalty companies:

- With dividend yields ranging from 10–15%
- Number of stocks = 4 (25% exposure to each stock / $5,000 per stock)
- Average weighted yield based on 4 specific stock choices = 12.5%
- Income = $2,500
- Potential capital appreciation = 4%
- Projected total return = Yield of 12.5% + capital appreciation of 4% = 16.5% of $20,000 = $3,300

Satellite portfolio – Growth & Income: $15,000 (15% of total capital invested) – quality stocks with average dividend yields of 2.5–3.0% and good capital appreciation prospects:

- Number of stocks = 3 (33% exposure / $5,000 per stock
- Average yield = 2.75%
- Income = $410
- Potential capital appreciation =10%
- Projected total return = Yield of 2.75% + capital appreciation of 10% = 12.75% of $15,000 = $1,910

Satellite portfolio – Growth: $15,000 (15% of total capital invested) – high growth stocks in higher risk sectors such as biotech with very good capital appreciation prospects:

- Number of stocks = 3 (33% exposure / $5,000 per stock)
- Average yield = 0%
- Income = 0%
- Potential capital appreciation = 20%
- Projected total return = No yield + capital appreciation of 20% = 20% of $15,000 = $3,000

Expected outcomes for the portfolio:

- Income = $5,410 = Yield return = 5.4%
- Projected capital Appreciation = $7,800 = Capital return = 7.8%
- Total return = $5,410 + $7,800 = $13,210 = 13.2%

Adjusting the portfolio

We have a problem! Our projection, based on what we believe to be realistic parameters, doesn't match our target of 15%; moreover, we haven't reality tested the projection by setting out some probabilities for our projected capital returns.

Clearly, we're not allocating enough capital to our growth satellite portfolios or we're being too conservative in terms of overall capital appreciation potential. Our projection for income (dividends) has a high probability of being achieved as long as circumstances allow us to hold those positions for a full year's worth of dividend payments. Hence, the variable in this equation is capital appreciation. And, it's a substantial variable, since unlike dividends, there's no relatively certain underlying support (corporate dividend policy is a very strong underlying support for income generation since companies really hate to decrease or suspend dividends except in significantly adverse situations such as those now being experienced by major oil and mining companies).

Here are our options.

1 In reviewing our portfolio structure we accept that our target was too high for the risk profile we want to achieve. In this case, the risk profile emphasizes income stocks and lower volatility income stocks. We've got 50% invested in high quality companies and another 20% in higher yielding income stocks. That leaves a very large return burden on the 30% of our capital allocated to growth

2 Perhaps our capital appreciation projection for our Core portfolio is too low? We've projected a total return for the Core of 10%, dividends plus price appreciation, and that total number is actually above the long-term total return average for the US stock market over a very long sample period. In terms of probabilities it would be an exceptional year in which our Core portfolio outperformed our projection. Fiddling at the edges here and raising the appreciation target could be self-delusory.

3 The only practical thing we can do to is to alter allocations. Put more money into the Growth satellite portfolios to hike our expected capital appreciation return. We are, however, also increasing our risk. In doing so do we still have an acceptable risk: reward ratio of say around 2: 1? This may be very hard to determine. All we can say for sure is that we are increasing our risk.

4 I think it's easy to see how we can tinker with the allocations to come up with altered outcomes. To prevent this review and potential adjustment process from becoming a nonsense exercise, let's consider the following points:

   a. In altering the allocations toward the higher risk satellite portfolios we may be getting outside our risk comfort level. Can we do this intelligently?

   b. Yes, in principle, we can.

i. We can set tighter stop loss levels for our riskier positions.

ii. There is a conundrum here – "riskier" stocks are defined as those with higher standard deviations of price movement (greater volatility). Hence, tighter stops have a greater chance of being hit for these higher volatility positions and this isn't useful. We'll just get knocked out of our positions as a result of the ordinary swings in the stock's price.

iii. We have to set our stops having looked at the stock's historic volatility to accommodate that "normal trading range". If we are not happy doing this because of volatility, we can't reallocate our overall portfolio towards greater risk.

There just aren't any miracle cures for real market conditions and limitations. If the investor behind this theoretical portfolio was young and gainfully employed, it could legitimately be argued that she / he can and should take greater risk and orient his portfolio from the outset of the structuring exercise towards greater reward for greater risk. The younger investor has got his or her current income, career prospects and time to recoup any early setbacks.

An older investor for whom capital conservation is the overarching goal would be best off accepting that his return goal of 15% was just not fully commensurate with his risk tolerance. That investor will be a lot better off collecting their current income and accepting lower capital returns rather than losing 15% or 20% of their capital. A lot better off operating within their risk tolerance using good money management, good capital allocation and Risk Management than getting themselves into a higher risked situation where lots of self-defeating, negative emotions will kick in if a downturn in the market or the more aggressive satellite portfolios occur. Negative emotions will always exacerbate losses.

This may seem obvious to many readers, but I can't emphasize too strongly the investment maxim that higher returns only come with higher risk. It's just unrealistic to expect big gains from low-risk investments. Of course, it can happen, but with about the frequency of winning the lottery (ok, better than 14 million to 1, but not by a lot).

There is nothing inherently wise, noble or useful in taking risks you cannot manage. It might appear macho, exciting or romantic, but it's truly a fool's game. What constitutes a reasonable risk for a tightrope walker would be just suicide, plain and simple, for me. Besides being nervous about heights, I have a poor sense of balance and no training or experience on a tightrope. What would be the glory, romance or machismo about that kind of risk for me?

Last point; Paul Tudor Jones, a near-legendary commodities and futures trader, doesn't try to deny fear or risk when trading. Quite the opposite: he succeeds because he accepts his fear and respects the risk, and the way he manages those things is to approach every trading idea with an initial review and continuing review of all the things that can go wrong with his trade.

A cautionary note

A problem with any analytical process and familiarity with the relevant analytical tools is always the risk of over-analysis (and under-action). We all have to figure out for ourselves when to stop analyzing something, when the "marginal utility" of further analysis starts to decline. There's no doubt that the PC and programs like Excel have entrapped many of us into endless analysis. It's so easy to do! And even entertaining for a while as an exercise for its own sake.

The point of having structured and analyzed / reviewed and possibly adjusted your portfolio or your expectations about the portfolio is that that structure is now a plan, and plans help you to interpret and deal with market realities.

A Prussian general said that no battle plan ever survives the beginning of a battle. I think we all know the inherent truth in this statement from our myriad life experiences. When the facts change we need to change our opinions (read, plans). No Prussian general, however, was ever going to enter a battle or a campaign without a plan.

As many readers will know (and as quoted in the film 'Wall Street') the Chinese philosopher-general Sun Tsu said that every battle is decided before the commencement of fighting. It's decided based on plans and the preparations called for by those plans and contingencies for those plans made by the victor prior to battle. I don't think Sun Tsu ever assumed that his plans were or should be immutable, but you need a plan.

Chapter 5

Idea Generation

One of the guiding principles of this book and the investment process described in it is pragmatism. The central argument of this book is that we have to take responsibility for our investments and for the growth and conservation of capital. And to do this we have to be realistic and pragmatic.

If you have a financial education or if financial analysis is your vocation, and furthermore you have the time and inclination, you can do your own investment research, your own idea generation and analysis. Many financial analytic tools, such as Discounted Fair Value, are a lot easier to do than many people think. But it can be time-consuming, it does involve a reasonable competency at reading / interpreting and manipulating company accounts, and it involves making lots of assumptions and adjustments.

This process is not practical for the majority of private investors – time and inclination probably being the main hurdles for most people.

I want to set out below two processes, both very "pragmatic" for investment idea generation. The two processes are not at all exclusive, and they can serve as a check and balance on each other. The first process involves the use of screening programs; the second, the use of analysts' newsletters.

These processes are practical for investors with a reasonable degree of financial sophistication, e.g. familiarity with the equity market and the range of basic financial principles and trading and investment strategies. All of these competencies can be acquired by individual investors through books or adult education courses and through online financial training sites.

Process 1: Screening: the steps and the outcome

This involves using the screening programs widely available on financial websites and quite possibly your broker's website. Some websites make screening exceptionally easy because they provide formatted options for screening using the different principal investment strategies. Screening programs simply scan the stock market and select out specific stocks that meet the screen criteria that either is pre-formatted or that you have set for the program.

Screening programs give you evaluation categories to choose from; such as price: earnings ratio, dividend yield, various growth parameters, and so on. You do not have to utilize every category offered, and within each category there's often a drop-down menu of values you can choose from as a limiting factor within the category.

In the UK, there is a very good website called Stockopedia. Stockopedia has a focus on what it calls "guru strategies". It has a number of pre-formatted screening options which use the investment parameters developed by "guru" investors: well-known, successful investors and all the major investment strategy categories: Growth, Value, Momentum and so on.

All of these screening programs allow you to develop a list of stocks matching the criteria that define the various strategies or using your own criteria. If you are comfortable selecting your own parameters, then you should do that. If you are not comfortable doing that, if you're not sure of the correct or effective criteria to use or you want to see an alternative to your own efforts, then use the pre-formatted screens where the website has selected the criteria to be applied.

Beyond Stockopedia there are other sites, possibly your broker's website, which offer screening. Additional sites (some of which may be free, other require you paying a subscription) are Yahoo Finance, Marketwatch.com, Meetinvest.com, MoneyAM, Investors Chronicle and others.

A cautionary word: Many website pre-formatted screens do not use sufficiently "discriminating parameters" and hence are prone to produce stock lists that are flawed in that many of the stocks selected only nominally meet the full definition of the strategy. A simple and common example:

I often use dividend-based screens looking for high yielding stocks for income. Some screening programs that are not sufficiently discriminating will produce stock choices that have high yields but are otherwise very flawed choices. Why? Some of the selected stocks have high yields because the criteria used were the last dividend paid and the current "depressed" stock price, thus producing a high yield. The danger here is that the company is in distress or performing poorly and is high risk and unlikely to continue to be able to pay a dividend at past levels, or any dividend at all.

In trying to identify good, high yielding stocks ancillary criteria are needed such as "dividend cover", which is the ratio of either net income or cash flow to the dividend. You would normally want to see dividend cover of at least 1.5:1 (depending on the nature of company, its history, its industry, its core business operations).

It is important to know what the pre-formatted screening programs' criteria are so you can be aware of the program's strengths or shortcomings.

With regard to Stockopedia, for example, it uses / replicates the parameters developed by leading investors and analysts. Assuming the criteria has been replicated accurately, you have a tool that is rigorous and proven over time as to the quality / effectiveness of the parameters used.

Screening is simply the most efficient way of independently generating investment ideas. It is what investors and analysts have been doing for 100 years but now, thanks to computers and the Internet, screening can be done by every investor.

Process 2: Analysts' newsletters

Many readers may well be skeptical about using equity market newsletters (or magazines) as sources of ideas and analysis. Some readers may well think it's somehow lazy or inappropriate to use newsletters (the work of others), but the reality is:

1 There are lots of very professional newsletters with reputable authors and excellent, independently determined track records.

2 Newsletter writers often have the expertise, the experience and the staffs and data sources to do excellent analysis. Analyses that are often well explained so that you can agree or disagree with both the methodology and the recommendation.

Newsletter writing has changed enormously since I began as an investor over 40 years ago. This is particularly true in the UK where old newsletters were amateur, rumor-based tip-sheets using entirely unprofessional and unsound processes for picking stocks.

Contemporary newsletters in the both the US and UK are now largely professionally written and researched; they are not tip-sheets and they are not vehicles for manipulating the price of penny stocks and pink sheet traded shares.

Just as the efficacy of various investment strategies varies over time and with market conditions, so does the performance and immediate utility of newsletters, all of which tend to focus on certain market sectors and / or certain investment strategies.

Newsletter pricing varies enormously. Many have very reasonable annual subscriptions varying from $150 –$500 for example. This is a cheap price for good quality investment advice. Remember, advice can't always be right; what also counts is the quality of the research that went into to trying to make an investment recommendation.

There are other letters which are hyped with subscriptions ranging up to $3,000 pa.

Are such letters grossly overpriced? Unfortunately, that's often something that can only be determined in retrospect and to some degree the price you can sensibly pay has a lot to do with the size of your investable capital, since that will in part determine the odds for making back the cost of the service on an annual basis.

I'm going to recommend some newsletters. I have no financial or personal relationship with any of them. I am paid subscriber to some. I have read them and I think they have merit, partly because of their results and partly because of the perceived quality and utility of their analytical processes.

Newsletter writers can often write in a somewhat exaggerated or overly-enthusiastic style – the quality of the rhetoric is often something to look beyond; rather the reader should focus on the analysis provided and determine if they think the analysis is reasonably rigorous, balanced and professional, or not. Newsletter rhetoric is also meant to be engaging and entertaining and some newsletter writers are somewhat eccentric.

Eccentricity by no means equates to incompetent or "dodgy". I think there is something about the newsletter writing process and the lifestyle of many of the writers that attracts eccentrics. Many writers were Wall Street analysts but left because either they became disillusioned with the financial services industry, or were entrepreneurial and wanted to work on their own and control their work environment.

Newsletters can be excellent sources for idea generation. Letters that focus on specific sectors such as natural resources are often written by authors who have worked in the sector, have relevant degrees such as petroleum engineering and who are also financial analysts. These letters can provide excellent background information and informed commentary about interesting sectors and can make stock selections within those sectors that are the product of useful experience in the specific sector.

As you the reader may already be aware institutional investors (hedge funds, pension funds, mutual funds et al) pay in one manner or another for research and stock selection recommendations from brokerage houses, investment banks and independent research companies. Those institutional investors rely on that research along with in-house research. They use it to see alternative ideas and differing opinions. They use it to take advantage of the industry-specific experience and expertise of the analysts.

If institutions with all their resources use outside research why wouldn't we? We most often cannot get the same research institutional investors can afford to buy, even when we have a brokerage account at the same broker the professional investor uses. Not surprisingly, there is one level of research for the peasants, another, and us for the nobles (the institutions).

Good quality newsletters are our outside research source. Good quality newsletters can be as wholly competent as high priced institutional in-house and purchased research.

One of the core principles of this book is that we can model ourselves after the best practices of successful professional investors. Modeling anything to improve our performance or quality of life does not mean and cannot mean doing exactly what our "model" does simply because we will often not have the resources or ability to strictly mimic our model.

This fact of life in no way denigrates or invalidates the concept and process of modeling. We go to the gym, sometimes use a trainer to show us best practice and appropriate exercise regimes for what we want to accomplish for ourselves.

Can I "mimic" the trainer with a 100% overlay? No, I can't. But does modeling ourselves after what the trainer does and recommends do us good? If practiced consistently and honestly, it does.

Modeling – approximating what successful investors do, using the resources available to us and using our capabilities in a disciplined and informed manner, will make us superior investors. Superior to the "crowd" and more importantly, superior to what we were in the past.

Set out below is a screen shot of a Fidelity Investment stock screen that I set up using a few parameters. It's easy to do. It's something you need to experiment with in order to understand the process and the mechanics of the program.

One thing you learn very quickly is how difficult it can be to generate your "ideal" stock selections. Depending on market conditions a value and income investor applying relatively strict criteria (yields above market medians, interest cover above market median, etc.) quickly discovers how few choices there are.

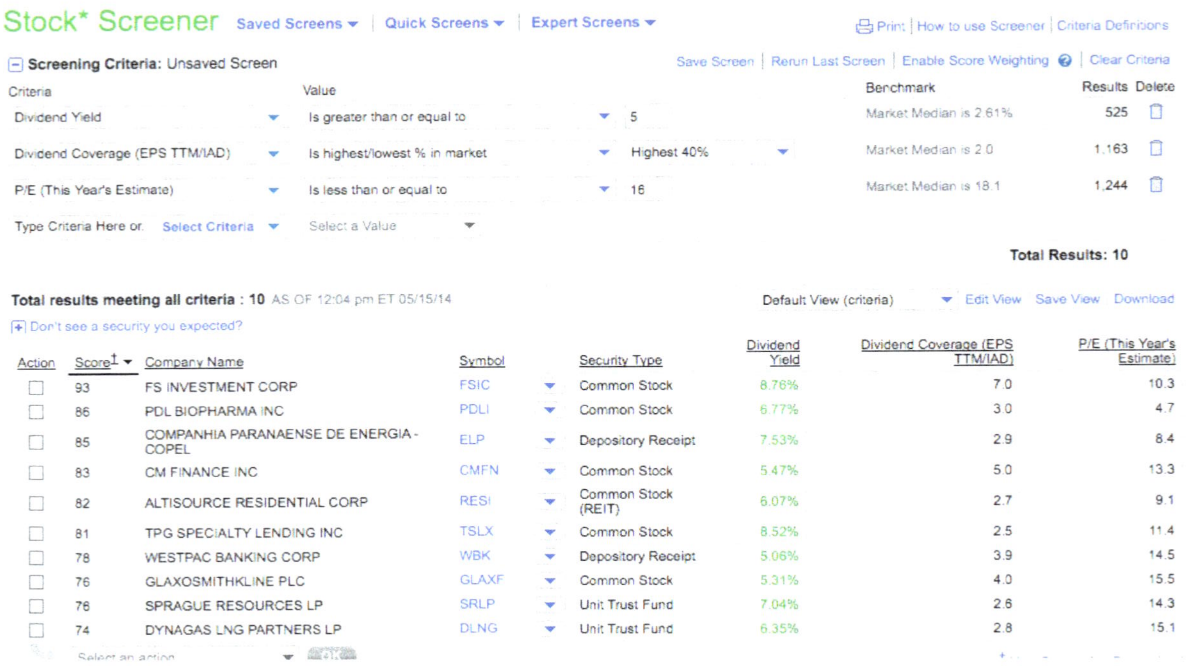

Stock* Screener Saved Screens Quick Screens Expert Screens

Print | How to use Screener | Criteria Definitions

Screening Criteria: Unsaved Screen

Save Screen | Rerun Last Screen | Enable Score Weighting | Clear Criteria

Criteria	Value		Benchmark	Results	Delete
Dividend Yield	Is greater than or equal to	5	Market Median is 2.61%	525	
Dividend Coverage (EPS TTM/IAD)	Is highest/lowest % in market	Highest 40%	Market Median is 2.0	1,163	
P/E (This Year's Estimate)	Is less than or equal to	16	Market Median is 18.1	1,244	
Type Criteria Here or Select Criteria	Select a Value				

Total Results: 10

Total results meeting all criteria : 10 AS OF 12:04 pm ET 05/15/14

Default View (criteria) Edit View Save View Download

Don't see a security you expected?

Action	Score	Company Name	Symbol	Security Type	Dividend Yield	Dividend Coverage (EPS TTM/IAD)	P/E (This Year's Estimate)
	93	FS INVESTMENT CORP	FSIC	Common Stock	8.76%	7.0	10.3
	86	PDL BIOPHARMA INC	PDLI	Common Stock	6.77%	3.0	4.7
	85	COMPANHIA PARANAENSE DE ENERGIA - COPEL	ELP	Depository Receipt	7.53%	2.9	8.4
	83	CM FINANCE INC	CMFN	Common Stock	5.47%	5.0	13.3
	82	ALTISOURCE RESIDENTIAL CORP	RESI	Common Stock (REIT)	6.07%	2.7	9.1
	81	TPG SPECIALTY LENDING INC	TSLX	Common Stock	8.52%	2.5	11.4
	78	WESTPAC BANKING CORP	WBK	Depository Receipt	5.06%	3.9	14.5
	76	GLAXOSMITHKLINE PLC	GLAXF	Common Stock	5.31%	4.0	15.5
	76	SPRAGUE RESOURCES LP	SRLP	Unit Trust Fund	7.04%	2.6	14.3
	74	DYNAGAS LNG PARTNERS LP	DLNG	Unit Trust Fund	6.35%	2.8	15.1

Select an action

Chart courtesy of Fidelity Investments

The screen shot set out below is a Fidelity "Expert Screen", the Low Price and High Projected Growth screen. This Expert Screen was chosen from among a list of Expert Screens and all the screening criteria were pre-formatted, as were the values for each criterion. You can change the values for each criterion and you get a different outcome in terms of stocks selected by the program. In using either a pre-formatted or custom (self-made) screen, you can match your chosen values against the program's benchmarks, set out in this instance on the right-hand side of the chart.

By comparing values, yours and market medians, you can see if your values are sensible or realistic. You can also then set values above or below market medians depending on your views about the market or individual sectors, or your own risk tolerance.

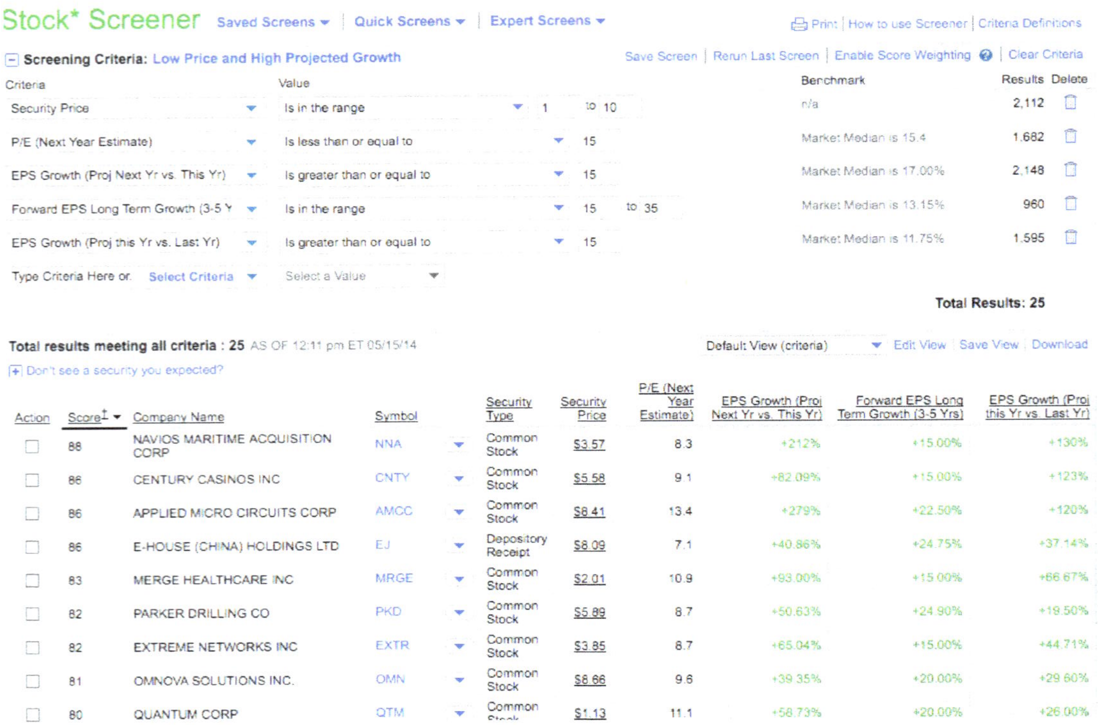

Stock* Screener Saved Screens ▾ | Quick Screens ▾ | Expert Screens ▾

Print | How to use Screener | Criteria Definitions

Screening Criteria: Low Price and High Projected Growth

Save Screen | Rerun Last Screen | Enable Score Weighting | Clear Criteria

Criteria	Value			Benchmark	Results	Delete
Security Price	Is in the range	1	to 10	n/a	2,112	
P/E (Next Year Estimate)	Is less than or equal to	15		Market Median is 15.4	1,682	
EPS Growth (Proj Next Yr vs. This Yr)	Is greater than or equal to	15		Market Median is 17.00%	2,148	
Forward EPS Long Term Growth (3-5 Y	Is in the range	15	to 35	Market Median is 13.15%	960	
EPS Growth (Proj this Yr vs. Last Yr)	Is greater than or equal to	15		Market Median is 11.75%	1,595	
Type Criteria Here or Select Criteria	Select a Value					

Total Results: 25

Total results meeting all criteria : 25 AS OF 12:11 pm ET 05/15/14

Default View (criteria) | Edit View | Save View | Download

[+] Don't see a security you expected?

Action	Score	Company Name	Symbol	Security Type	Security Price	P/E (Next Year Estimate)	EPS Growth (Proj Next Yr vs. This Yr)	Forward EPS Long Term Growth (3-5 Yrs)	EPS Growth (Proj this Yr vs. Last Yr)
☐	88	NAVIOS MARITIME ACQUISITION CORP	NNA	Common Stock	$3.57	8.3	+212%	+15.00%	+130%
☐	86	CENTURY CASINOS INC	CNTY	Common Stock	$5.58	9.1	+82.09%	+15.00%	+123%
☐	86	APPLIED MICRO CIRCUITS CORP	AMCC	Common Stock	$8.41	13.4	+279%	+22.50%	+120%
☐	86	E-HOUSE (CHINA) HOLDINGS LTD	EJ	Depository Receipt	$8.09	7.1	+40.86%	+24.75%	+37.14%
☐	83	MERGE HEALTHCARE INC	MRGE	Common Stock	$2.01	10.9	+93.00%	+15.00%	+66.67%
☐	82	PARKER DRILLING CO	PKD	Common Stock	$5.89	8.7	+50.63%	+24.90%	+19.50%
☐	82	EXTREME NETWORKS INC	EXTR	Common Stock	$3.85	8.7	+65.04%	+15.00%	+44.71%
☐	81	OMNOVA SOLUTIONS INC.	OMN	Common Stock	$8.66	9.6	+39.35%	+20.00%	+29.60%
☐	80	QUANTUM CORP	QTM	Common Stock	$1.13	11.1	+58.73%	+20.00%	+26.00%

Chart courtesy of Fidelity Investments

The next screen shot is a partial shot of the Stockopedia "Guru Screen" page. This screening program lets you chose from either a selection of investment styles or the strategies used by specific investors of note. The output is automatically correlated to the parameters that Stockopedia uses to define the various investment styles and investor-specific strategies.

Using the screens, you can either mimic a style or investor strategy or develop your own modifications in terms stocks chosen.

It is important to remember that this is not a static process. It's a dynamic process that has to be monitored and rebalanced over the course of the investing year. As market conditions change, as company information is updated and stock prices change, the screens are going to produce different results because some stocks will drop out of the criteria range and others may now enter into it. You've got to check at least once a quarter – not a big deal in terms of time spent.

The same of course is true for a custom screen for all the same reasons. Things change and as the facts change we will want to change our opinions and hence our portfolio components.

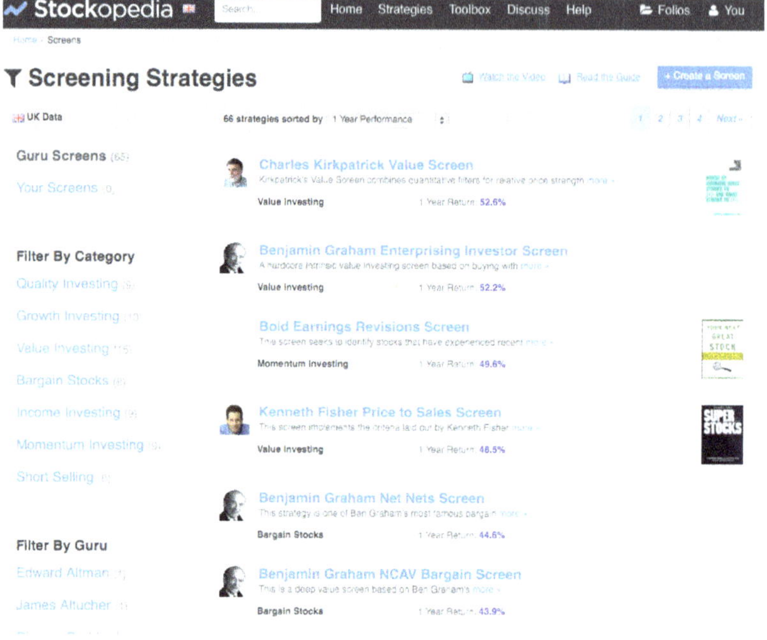

Chart courtesy of Stockopedia

Equity newsletters

In the world of US equity newsletters there are two main publishers, Stansberry and Agora. Each publisher distributes a number of proprietary equity newsletters, some of which are sector-specific such as natural resources. Both publishers have websites and in viewing them you can see the range of letters published.

Additionally, there are publishers who aggregate and distribute the work of independent analysts and writers. They provide an administrative and marketing service for the individual authors.

Many newsletter writers and publishers have a political bent, several being Libertarians or quasi-libertarians. Newsletter writers tend to have strong political opinions that they often can't help voicing (and are often criticized by readers for doing so). Some writers are downright eccentric but nonetheless in terms of stock picking and analysis wholly competent. Some publications are technically oriented, limiting their verbiage and focusing strongly on quantitative analysis of the market.

Without specific recommendation listed below are a number of publications that I think are good quality and useful. Some are better written than others and some certainly more amusing than others.

In the US:

- True Wealth – Steve Sjuggerud
- Turner Analytics and Signal Investor – Mike Turner
- Capital and Crisis – Chris Mayer
- Arora – Nigram Arora
- Outstanding Investor (natural resources) – Brian Hunt
- Richard Band, Profitable Investing
- Retirement Investor – David Eifrig
- Strategic Investor – Addison Wiggin
- Various Cabot publication newsletters (value, growth, dividend)

In the UK:

- Trendwatch – Rob Cullum
- Investors' Chronicle
- Shares Magazine
- Momentum Investor
- Money Week

In addition to newsletters and magazines there are other services that don't make specific stock recommendations but are information sources on the sectors they cover. Some very good examples are:

- Stockopedia – UK
- Dividend Max
- Dividend.com – USA
- ETFDB – USA

If you are particularly interested (as I am) in investment trusts I can recommend two resources:

- *Money Observer* magazine, with covers the sector and has excellent statistical / performance data for a huge range of investment trusts;
- Trustnet.com, which covers both unit trusts and investment trusts.

These sites can be enormously useful in terms of idea generation, risk assessment and management and information on the mechanics of dividends, stock strategies and ETFs.

A couple of points of caution about equity newsletters:

- Newsletter writers are largely expected by their publishers and readers to generate stock selections in every edition of the publication. Good writers don't do this and this is a good basis for judging the intellectual honesty and the utility of many newsletters.
- Once you subscribe to a newsletter you will either get lots of solicitations for other letters or the solicitations from the letter's publisher to "upgrade" your service, or join their exclusive club of investors. Newsletter writers and publishers are business people and they are going to keep "pushing the envelope" with their subscribers. Be prepared, but remember, the value of the letter is not diminished by the commercial machinations of its author or publisher; you need look past this behavior and focus on the quality of the analysis and information in the letter itself.

Watch lists

Your broker's website plus many other websites, several of which have already been cited, enable you construct "watch list" portfolios of stocks you are interested in tracking. The benefit of website watch list functionality is the automated updating of price information intra-day and over time.

I am a big user of watch lists. Having identified through any number of resources stocks, funds, trusts that interest me. I load them on to various "themed" or dated watch lists. Nothing could be easier. Nothing could be more useful. Why?

Rather than immediately acting on an idea, particularly when you are relying on the opinion of others (no matter how professional they may be) it's really useful to first track the proposed investment and watch the price action.

I review my watch lists frequently. What I'm looking for is simply those investment ideas with momentum. I want to see evidence of upward momentum before I commit. I may well wait until a specific investment has risen 5% or 7% (over days or a few weeks) before committing.

Set up some watch lists yourself of recommend / highly recommended investments from a variety of quality sources and you will see a very interesting divisions in performance post those recommendations. Which is the prime reason for watching, waiting and seeing.

We are often prone to want to jump into an investment immediately upon learning about it and reviewing it. But take it from Nathan Rothschild: "Always leave the last penny of profit to next fellow". In other words, don't be greedy and emotionally driven to dive into an untested investment opportunity and don't be greedy in holding on beyond reasonable upside performance either.

Summary

If we follow the news and if we are able to sum up our own personal financial situation and understand our own goals and risk tolerance, we will have "views" on the types of investments we want to make, the sectors we are likely to be interested in. Using the resources we've discussed in this chapter enables us to hone our research efforts, to discover other views and new investment ideas.

Whatever sources you chose to use or exclude, a key criterion is your situation, your goals, your risk tolerance and your investment management capabilities and time commitment.

Chapter 6

Defensive Investing Rules

Everybody likes rules! Unfortunately, rules seem to be made to at least be bent, if not broken. The good thing about rules is at a minimum they give us something to reflect on which can help us to evolve ranges within which we can successfully operate. Reviewing rules gives us a chance to reflect on the market and our investment attitudes and activities.

Six main rules

There are lots of stock market rules and sometimes rules from different sources can be annoyingly contradictory. But, nonetheless, here are a few worthwhile rules. I have excerpted some of these rules from Shares magazine (May 15, 2014 edition) a very good quality UK weekly equity magazine. The comments attendant to the rules set out below are mine.

1. **Set a clear goal** for your investing activities. We've referenced this in Chapter 1. The key points worth reflecting on and writing down are:

    a. Why am I investing – which means: what am I trying to achieve, what is my annual return target, what's my risk tolerance. What it is that you are trying to achieve can be stated in terms of what is it you want the capital for, and hence how much capital you will need. Don't set arbitrary money goals, link the amount to something tangible that you want to get, that you will need to pay for.

b. You will have to revise your goals. As the facts change, as your life changes, you need to review and potentially change your goals and hence alter your investment style. Reviewing and revising is reality testing; it is not a form of excuse setting or making downward revisions to goals because you're having problems attaining them. It is in part an examination of what problems you may be having and what you need to do to correct them.

2 **Seek out firms with competitive advantages.** If you're familiar with Warren Buffet, then you know that this is essentially his core investment philosophy. It's of course a lot easier said than done, particularly if you want to identify emerging or evolving companies. It's easy, but not without error, to just pick the Dow Industrial Average constituent stocks – there are just 30 of them.

a. I think where this rule can be really useful and best employed is in choosing between several investment options. Your research, your reading, has come up with two or more companies to consider. You want to decide on one or maybe two stocks at most. One good criterion to apply is: which of the options appears to be a company with a strong competitive advantage? Which is the industry / market leader? Which company has a strong "brand identity"?

b. If you want to invest for the longer term and if you want to hold a limited number of positions you do need to focus on this rule.

3. **Know your limits.** This is all about knowing your risk tolerance and operating within it. Going back to Warren Buffet again, he has said that if an investor lacks the confidence to research and make his own investment choices, then a good alternative is to invest in a managed index fund such as an S&P 500 tracker fund. That way the investor cedes

responsibility to professional management, knowing that the manager is simply going to replicate ownership of the 500 largest US listed companies that compose this index.

a. Risk tolerance. We've said you need to know your risk tolerance. How do you determine this? Just be honest with yourself, no macho stuff, and ask yourself the following question:

   i. I have $xxx of capital (say $100,000). How much could I lose (realized or unrealized losses) before I got really worried / upset / disillusioned with investments / lost my self-confidence / felt awful / felt guilty, and so on. Is it $5,000 or $7,500 or $10,000, etc.?

   ii. If you find it hard to set a loss number you feel strongly about try this: don't think in dollar terms, think first about what that lost capital could have bought you – something you value, e.g.

      - A year's worth of mortgage payments;
      - A new car;
      - A particularly desired vacation;
      - A year's school fees and so on.

   iii. Once you've come up with a number, you can then use it when framing your Risk Management program. You will use that number to set your money management plan and your stop loss levels such that you will not lose more than that risk tolerance amount in any investment year.

4 Prioritize cash flow over accounting profits. When doing your research, and whether you have been given the numbers by an equity newsletter or you've taken them off a financial website, focus on a company's cash flow, not its accounting net income before or after tax. Why?

a Because cash is real, cash is king, and as was said in old Brooklyn, "money talks, nobody walks".

b Neither companies nor families can survive without a positive cash flow. Countries can get away with this for a long time to the extent they can print money others will accept. Companies and families can cope for a while by borrowing, but then the underlying reality of their inability to generate cash flow other than from borrowing will really undo them

c Focus on ratios using cash flow; price: cash flow; enterprise value: free cash flow for the year; cash flow cover of dividends paid; cash flow to debt repayments.

If you can't or don't want to do this type of numerical analysis then just pay special attention to a write-up on a company (or sometimes even a sector) where the author / analyst is expressing either concern or a positive view with regard to a company's cash flow generation versus its (non-cash) accounting profit.

1 **Buy low and sell high.** Which really means: just don't do what so many private investors do – don't buy at the top of a market and then end up selling into the bottom after the crash. Easier said than done? Yes and no.

   a If you do your reading and research, if you stay aware of the world around you, you will read a lot about whether we're at or heading fast to a market top or a market bottom. There's no guarantee about the acumen or timing accuracy of what you will read, but the benefit of what you read is that it can serve as a warning and a warning to be heeded.

   b You can heed a warning by simply not plunging into a market when it is clearly reaching multi-year highs. Moderation in everything – you can "shade" into the market using only a limited amount of your capital and buying only high quality, non-speculative and non-momentum-only driven stocks.

c To be a successful long-term investor you do not have to buy at the low and sell at the high – when a market is in a bull run there's lots of time to get into it advantageously and then to let your profits run and eventually cut your losses (sell on major market retreats).

2 **Stay aware of the big picture.** We can't invest in vacuum; we have to be aware of the bigger world of economics, politics, and market sentiment. And we have to factor that information flow into what we are reading and hearing about the investment markets so that we can modify our strategy and tactics according to how we believe the environment will impact the stock market.

Expectations

A good context for rule setting and managing our behaviors in accordance with our rules is to have realistic expectations for stock market performance. You can find lots of studies / estimates for stock market price appreciation over time for the major markets such as the US and the UK.

What you will see is a range of numbers, sometimes quite wide. Diverging historical numbers have everything to do with:

- The time range of the study;
- Whether the study focuses on total annual return or just price appreciation alone;
- "Evidential" problems when you go way back in time and find lots of data gaps and sometimes have to use proxy numbers.

As far as return projections are concerned, there's always a range of outlooks to be found. But note:

- When major bank economists and analysts are asked by a newspaper to project the coming year's stock market performance, you will often see a lot "clustering" around a mean in the projections. Why? Because competing bank analysts and economists don't want to look foolish. If they're going to be wrong they want to be wrong with the crowd and not as an outlier.
- Projections are often entirely subjective and when investment managers are polled you will quite understandably get a projection that reflects their strategy and beliefs, if they are prepared to go out on a limb and assert their genuine views. Right now a couple of major investment managers are projecting very low annual returns for the major stock markets over the next decade due to their view of the impact of central bank policies and economic growth in the developed world. They may be right, they may be wrong, but you can at least understand the reasoning underlying their projections and their biases.
- Reversion to the mean. Like the bell-shaped curve, reversion to the mean is one of those universal phenomena of the world we live in. What it means is that, over time, an event, such as stock market annual performance, will revert to its mean, its long- term average. Now, that doesn't mean life is static. The average can and does change over time, but what it does mean is that if the average annual growth in the Dow Jones Average over the last 100 years was, say, 8% and over the next several years we had growth of only, say, 4%, eventually annual market performance will revert back up to around 8%.

  The practical importance of this phenomenon is that if the mean return for stocks in the Dow was, say, 8%, then for long term (and I stress long term: 10, 20, 30 years) we can have some statistically robust confidence that it's probable that the next 20 or so years will produce a similar outcome (not an exact replica) and hence for planning purposes, it's not unreasonable to use that historic number as base planning case. But remember time lags. If you are planning over say 10 years, and the outlook for the next 3–5 years is say 4% and then a possible reversion to the mean 8% thereafter then you will not achieve an 8% average over the 10 years.

Historic Dow Jones Index returns

Source: http://www.observationsandnotes.blogspot.co.uk

Average stock market return per year: last 5, 10, 20 ... years

- The long-term, more than 100-year performance: since 1900 (end-of-year 1899), through 2012, the average annual total return of the DJIA (Dow Jones Industrial Average) was approximately 9.4% – 4.8% in price appreciation, plus approximately 4.6% in dividends. (Some numbers may not add up due to rounding.)
- Since 1929 (year-end 1928 – i.e., before the 1929 stock market crash), through 2012, the return was 8.8% (4.6%, plus 4.2%). Since end-of-year 1932 (i.e., after the crash): 11.1% (7.0%, plus 4.2%).
- The average annual stock market return for the past 25 calendar years (since 1987) was 10.6% (7.9%, plus 2.7%).
- Stock market returns for the 20 years (since 1992): 9.6% (7.1%, plus 2.4%) In the middle of one of the longest bull markets in history. (See below for additional 20-year periods.)
- Returns since 1999 (13 years) – the dot.com bubble year-end peak: 3.4% (1.0%, plus 2.4%).

- Returns for the 10 years (since 2002): 7.2% (4.6%, plus 2.6%); year-end trough after the dot.com bubble. (See below for additional 10-year periods.)
- For the 5 years (since 2007), 2.6% (-0.2%, plus 2.8%) year-end peak of housing bubble.
- Since 2008 year-end trough after the housing bubble: 13.4% (10.5%, plus 2.9%).
- For 2012 the stock market (Dow/DJIA) total return was 10.1% (7.3% plus 2.9%);
  - 2012 year-end dividend yield was 2.7%.

The table set out below was devised by StockPicksSystem and shows returns on the Dow Jones Index from the 1900s to 2013.

Decade	Return
1900s	9.96%
1910s	4.20%
1920s	14.95%
1930s	-0.63%
1940s	8.72%
1950s	19.28%
1960s	7.78%
1970s	5.82%
1980s	17.57%
1990s	18.17%
2000s	1.07%
2010-2013	16.74%

S&P 500 Index since 2012	
2015	1.30
2014	13.81
2013	32.43

Looking at the information set out above you can see:

1 A big variance in performance over various discrete time frames.

2 You can clearly see the importance of dividends as a component of total return.

3 The variance in performance over different time frames shows how important it is to be a longer-term investor; that way you can play something akin to the "law of large numbers" and have a better chance of achieving good results.

If you were starting out today as an investor, which of the return numbers shown above would you want to use for planning purposes? There is no easy answer to this but the return number for the period 2002–2012 would be a reasonably valid choice. Why? Because it has to be more reflective of the world we now live in and all that entails in terms of central bank policy, politics and economics. Another good thing about that period for planning purposes is that it encompasses the big 2007–09 financial crisis bust and the subsequent recovery. This adds a meaningful dimension of "market realism" to the period and the return number.

As a check, look at the number for the period 1929–2012. Here we have a very long-term return number that is 1.6% absolute above the shorter period number. A relatively big difference on the upside, but nonetheless we now have two numbers and a useful time difference in those numbers. And both sets of numbers include some big ups and some big downs. The long-term number has the statistical benefit of including a lot more ups and downs and hence can be said to be a more reliable statistic for our planning purposes.

Now we have a basis for planning, we have a "numerically expressed expectation" for potential, long-term gains. Additionally, we also have a clear indication of how important dividends are in achieving investment success.

Dividend reinvestment

Dividend reinvestment is exactly what it says. Rather than taking your dividends in cash, you reinvest in the company that paid them, you buy more shares. Most brokers have dividend reinvestment functionality that allow you to automatically reinvest dividends paid, and such plans are often done in conjunction with company you've received the dividend from. The reason for these plans is to minimize or eliminate brokerage fees when you buy the additional shares.

Dividend reinvestment can be a great long-term strategy. Again, studies have shown conclusively, hugely different and better returns over 20- and 30-year periods when dividend reinvestment is continually employed. I can vouch for this; back in the 1980s through the mid1990s I reinvested most (not all) of my dividends and benefited considerably from owning more of a portfolio of funds and stocks that grew during a prolonged bull market.

Dividend reinvestment is a tactic that younger investors should absolutely consider and engage in with part or all of their portfolio. When you have a 20–40-year time horizon. It is a process that can and should greatly enhance your capital

Specific investing rules

I've excerpted the four investing rules from the *Stansberry Digest*, Stansberry Publishing. The four rules set out below are clear and easy to apply if you are so minded.

Four Rules of Thumb to Collect Income and Grow Your Wealth Safely

By Dr. David Eifrig, author, *Big Book of Retirement Secrets*

Rule No. 1: Look for price-to-earnings (P/E) ratios below the long-term average of the S&P 500, generally below 17. A low P/E ratio suggests the company is trading below its value, making it cheap.

Rule No. 2: Look for stocks trading for a price-to-book (P/B) ratio below one. A low P/B value suggests the company is undervalued, and you could be getting into a great company at a discount.

Rule No. 3: Try to avoid paying more than a price-to-sales ratio of three for the stock of a solid, reliable business.

In the private markets, businesses usually get bought and sold at prices that are between one and two times sales. Of course, some well-established businesses with reliable sales can command a higher ratio.

Rule No. 4: Look for stocks that pay a dividend representing at least 2% of the share price. I also like to see a history of growing dividend payments. And I like the dividend yield to exceed the five-year Treasury note.

Simple rules of investment behavior

Now, I want to add and reiterate some simple but critical rules of investing behavior.

1. **Don't ever panic.** No matter how tough or scary the market may get, think first and act as prudently as you can. No easy rule to implement, but let me suggest that in situations where you find yourself prone to panic, turn off the PC and walk away from the TV set – leave the market to its own devices. This is not being irresponsible or sticking your head in the sand. It is separating yourself from the crowd, giving yourself time to calm down, reflect and plot a sensible response. Also note that, not always, but frequently, a major market down day is follow by an equal or almost equal sized recovery day. If you want to get out of a position or the market giving yourself some breathing space is often the best response

2. **Avoid panic in the first place by:**
   - Respecting your risk tolerance and not getting in over your head;
   - Using Money Management and stop losses.

3. **Don't over-trade.** On both the upside and the downside don't over-trade; don't get into a flurry of ill-considered buying and selling. You are very unlikely to do anything but exacerbate your losses when you start "panic trading".

4. **Don't average down.** Averaging down is the practice of buying more of a stock as its prices trends lower on the basis that this is a good way of recovering your initial losses when the stock eventually rises. Some sophisticated investors, having made a very strong conviction trade, will average down, telling you that the investment case hasn't changed for the worse just because the price has fallen and now you are being given a chance to hype your position and eventual gain at a bargain price.

Don't catch falling knives: if a stock is trending down, let it go, get out of it, particularly when you have no real insight into the company's operations. Averaging down is something desperate traders very often do, and it almost always ends in tears.

5 **As already mentioned:** don't buy at the top and sell at the bottom. This is the curse and the undoing of the unskilled and unreflective / reactive investor. As many of you readers will know, a major bear market signal for sophisticated investors arrives when market finally attracts big time small investor participation.

- Be patient, be inquisitive, and wait for the market when at a high to make new highs and then wait for several days to see if those new highs "stick" – wait for "confirmation". If the market or a stock doesn't have that kind of momentum, then it's made its high point and it is too late to get in sensibly.
- If you don't buy high then it is very unlikely you will end up selling low, particularly if you stick with our Risk Management rules and processes which will get you out way before any lows are hit.

6 **Do the "Zen thing".** Trade "quietly" and meditate on the market whenever you feel driven to just trade in order to take up a friend's tip or good advice or because you think market is moving onwards without you being sufficiently invested in it.

I know that the popular conception of investing / trading is driven by images of traders on the floor of various commodity exchanges yelling and frantically making hand signals. This kind of trading behavior is largely going the way of dial-up Internet and is being replaced by electronic trading. The point I want to make is that successful investors and traders do not engage in hectic, manic trading activity. Hedge funds, for example, along with other investment companies, have lots of analysts and trading assistants and spend lots of man-hours researching stocks and the market as a whole. This is also true for the major successful commodity traders and trading companies. The minute-to-minute changes in prices are "noise" to them. The reality is that many of those macho floor traders on commodity exchanges literally kill themselves trading price differences of a penny and are lucky to finish a grinding, exhausting day $300 ahead.

In 'the battle for investment survival', be a general – take the overview, the longer view and act strategically.

7 **The final rule: be consistent, be disciplined.** Follow your rules, use your Risk Management processes and when you find yourself bypassing these practices, **stop trading, rest, reflect and then resume when you once again are disciplined.**

Chapter 7

Investment Choices: Stocks, ETFs and Funds

There are several different categories of equity and bond instruments that you can use to construct a portfolio. There are some big differences in terms of risk and reward characteristics among these investment instruments. There are also a number of practical issues presented or resolved by the different instruments we can choose.

It would not at all be unusual to have a portfolio containing a mix of the different choices; each serves a purpose and can be successfully used to fine-tune a Core and Satellite portfolio structure. Very often these different instruments provide "solutions" to specific investment and portfolio problems.

It would be entirely possible to write a whole book on this topic examining each investment instrument in detail and doing a school essay of "compare and contrast". I don't want to do that and I don't think it's necessary for our purpose. Let's stick with some broad and very relevant issues. There are some significant differences between the UK and US here, and I will point them out as we go along.

Every one of these instruments can be researched easily and extensively online, so each reader can go far as they want to go in terms of information and detail.

Individual stocks

The great attraction of choosing an individual stock is the potential for outperformance, both of the market as a whole and the company's particular sector. We can focus on the particular risk and value metrics of the stock and we can make a clear choice of where we think the optimal investment potential lies. We can also easily follow that one stock and manage our position.

The downside of choosing an individual stock or a couple of stocks is limited diversification and, very importantly, we may find it very difficult to differentiate between several leading participants in a market sector and thus have no sound or confident basis for making individual stock selections or then subsequently managing them.

If you are for any reason uncomfortable with stock-picking (and I absolutely don't want you relying on the neighbour's tips) then so-called "collective investment schemes" such as mutual funds, investment trusts, unit trusts and ETFs are for you.

Mutual funds

There are a large number of mutual funds and their UK equivalent, unit trusts, to choose from – too many, actually. Funds can be actively managed or they can be "passive" in that they track various market indices such as the FTSE 100 or S&P 500 and many other indices. Funds can be sector-specific or they can focus on different geographic areas, specific national markets and investment style types such "large-cap", "mid-cap", "small cap", "value", "growth" and the many more variations are on offer.

Websites such as Morningstar in the US and the UK and many mutual fund newsletters analyse and rate funds and make recommendations.

Increasingly in the US, many funds have eliminated their front-end fees; in other words they no longer charge buying commissions that used to run to as much as 5% of your investment amount. Unfortunately, in the UK most unit trusts continue to charge hefty fees (the spread between their bid and offer prices) as well as high, continuing management fees that absolutely impact returns, particularly in sideways trending markets and down markets.

Tracker funds

As mentioned there are passive funds or "tracker funds"; these funds and unit trusts are and should be cheap to buy, with very low on-going management costs. The reason: these funds just invest in an index, whether it's the Dow or the FTSE or an industry sector composite. The funds are not actively managed; their key operating criteria is to have the lowest "tracking error" possible.

Frankly, there are even cheaper ways of tracking an index. Exchange Traded Funds (ETFs), explained below, are one way; in the UK, investment trust trackers can be another way.

I think the sole rationale for buying a fund is "active management". This is also true for a UK unit trust. What is the point of paying a management fee (and possibly an up-front fee) if you are not getting active management in terms of risk mitigation and reward optimization? I think there simply is no point. If you can risk-manage your investments using the tools we've discussed, you don't need a tracker fund.

The biggest problem for me with a tracker fund is that it will track its reference index: on the way up, great, but then it will do the same all the way down. Unless you see a value in riding a market down and watching your capital erode you are going to want to get out of the fund and you are going to use the Risk Management / capital conservation tools and techniques we've talked about to do so. So why not consider an actively managed fund where you may have a manager able to outperform the market as a whole and who will not just ride the index down passively in a bear market.

There has been a campaign among investors and investor organizations (starting in Sweden) and expanding into the UK to identify "closet tracker funds". These are funds that claim to be actively managed but in reality, their portfolios have 90% plus overlaps with their benchmarking indices. The problem here is that investors firstly think they are investing in an actively managed fund that aims to outperform their benchmark, and secondly they're paying active management level fees for passive / tracking performance.

Having "dissed" tracker funds I do want to make the following suggestion: if you believe that as a result of economic and political trends there is going to be a overall rise in the equity market and you do not feel capable making or taking the time to research funds, then "trading" a tracker fund for the principal indices such as the Dow, the S&P 500 or the Russell 2000 is a perfectly valid idea. I urge you to use our Risk Management tools and don't just ride a fund and its index down – go to cash instead. Follow the trend and then "trade" out of it. If you are able and interested to do the research, then look for actively managed funds, trusts and ETFs with good track records versus the main market indices.

Lastly on this subject: using a tracker fund as a hedge is a very valid idea. What you're hedging is your judgement. You construct your Core and Satellite portfolio with your choices of individual stocks, funds, ETFs etc., and balance your view with an index tracker that reflects the broader investor view of the market. What is also useful about this approach is that, using the tracker fund as a benchmark, you can compare (cannot avoid comparing) your performance against the market and you can make continuing adjustments to try to fine-tune your overall portfolio performance.

Some of you may have heard of the American investment manager, John Bogle, founder of the Vanguard funds and effectively the "father" of index tracker funds. Bogle who was an active manager concluded based on both experience and historical performance that passive tracker funds were investors' best choice for capital appreciation over the "long term". I would not take issue with Bogle though many of his active investment competitors have done so over many years. However, it is worth noting that a tracker fund can experience years of poor returns based on market conditions. Investors have to make decisions using time frames that sensible for them. A very long-term outlook is right if you 20 or 30 years old and not useful if your 65 or 75 years old. Age and individual financial circumstances are critical variables in evolving an investment strategy.

Most funds do not outperform the market as a whole. Sad, but true. But, there is that 5% of all fund investment managers who can outperform the market on a continuing basis. They are few in number, and no manager's winning streak goes on forever, but a number of managers can provide investors with market superior returns over several years. Fund managers are the subject of Appendix 10.

Your broker's website is very likely to have a screening program for mutual funds, ETFs and investment trusts which you can use to find better performing funds across all the fund investment style types. Your broker may just use Morningstar, and that's fine. There are also newsletters that specialize in funds and assemble model portfolios of funds for their subscribers. These letters track fund performance, analyse recommended funds and often rate them using their own proprietary system.

Investment trusts

In the UK an excellent alternative to unit trusts is the wide range of investment trusts. Investment trusts were created in the 19th Century and are “closed end investment companies”. A closed end investment company is a company that issues shares that are listed and traded on the London Stock Exchange. You buy and sell them just like any other stock. Closed end means that, barring the issue of new shares to the market; investors can only buy into a trust by buying them through the stock exchange.

If a trust wants to issue new shares it has to follow the same procedures set out for, say, Royal Dutch Shell or Diageo. Trusts can and do run share buy-back schemes, but all this means is that the trust, just like Royal Dutch, “enters” the market bidding to buy shares at a stated price.

A critical difference between unit trusts and investment trusts (open ended v closed end) is that the unit trust by charter and regulation stands ready to buy and sell (redeem and issue) its units (shares) every day. The problem here is that in a severe market downturn (and this has happened in the last 20 years) unit trusts have had to suspend the redemption of their units. This leaves investors out in the cold while watching the price (net asset value) of the units declining in reaction to the downturn in the unit trust’s holdings. Not a comfortable position to be in. The risk of suspension is much greater for specialist funds investing in more exotic, less liquid markets.

The advantage of an investment trust is that it doesn’t have to buy back its own shares. It only does so at its own discretion if the share price is at a large discount to the trust’s net asset value. In a market panic, you can sell your investment trust shares through the market (as long as there are would-be buyers), but the key point is that there is no suspension problem. This also allows the investment trust industry to create a wider range of specialist trusts which can include private equity investments and investments focused on less liquid markets (emerging markets, frontier markets, industry sectors, etc.) because they will not need to be forced sellers in a collapsing market in order to raise cash to redeem shares.

Mutual funds and unit trusts

What's the difference? As cited above, US mutual funds and UK unit trusts are open-ended investment companies responding to investor demand to buy or sell (redeem) their units every day or on set days.

To facilitate its investors buying or selling its units, the fund or unit trust will issue new units or buy them back. In the US, funds buy and sell at Net Asset Value (the value of all their investments divided by the number of outstanding shares). In the UK, unit trusts post bid and offer prices with a spread that can be as much as 4% or 5% and transact at those prices.

To be clear, investors can only buy shares or units from the fund or unit trust and can only sell back to the fund or unit trust; these collective investment schemes are not companies and they are not listed and traded on exchanges.

This means that, subject to the UK unit trust bid/offer spread, investors in unit trusts and mutual funds:

a Buy into and sell out of funds at about the real value of the funds' investment holdings (minus the spread between the buying and selling prices (bid and offer) and any upfront fee charged by a US fund.

b It also means that in market panics, fund redemptions can be denied and deferred. This happens because, in order to meet the redemption demand, the fund or unit trust manager has to sell the fund's underlying investments.

c In a market panic the fund may be unable to sell large blocks of its holding or unwilling to sell them because market conditions are so bad that fair and realistic prices for these underlying investments cannot be had. This can be problematic (and scary) for the investors who are trying to cut their losses and redeem their positions

The contrasting position of investment trusts (and US closed end funds)

When an investor wants to close out their position in an investment trust or a US closed end fund, the trust or fund doesn't "redeem" its stock; it actually doesn't do anything. Through his broker and the stock market the selling investor seeks a buyer at the market price for his or her shares just as he or she would if they selling Apple or British Land.

In a market panic, the trust or closed end fund is unaffected, directly unaffected by market conditions. The value of its investments may well go down and hence its net asset value and share price, but since it doesn't redeem stock it doesn't have to realize any of its underlying investments at possibly transitorily unsatisfactory and unrealistic prices.

Investment trusts and closed end funds do not levy up-front fees and they have much lower management fees than the average mutual fund or unit trust. But, the big issue for investment trusts is that they very often trade at a discount to their net asset value – this means the market price for the trust is less than the value of its underlying investments.

Why does this happen? Partly because of management fees, partly because the trust or closed end fund can trade in and out of its underlying investments at any time, thus making it hard to really know what the trust's positions and net asset value is on a day-to-day basis and the investor is at a remove from his investments. Meaning that when you invest in a trust or a closed end fund, you are buying into its underlying investments but you have no control or direct access to those underlying investments and you are "buying into" the quality of its management and their judgment and actions (you're doing the same with mutual funds and unit trusts, but those investments are not market traded and hence their prices are subject to different forces and different conventions).

Additionally and very importantly, trusts can borrow (from banks and other lenders) in order to leverage themselves and to try to hype returns on behalf of its shareholders. Leverage involves risk and it is also a factor in creating a discount from net asset value.

It's very attractive to buy net assets for less than their net worth. A potential attraction of investment trusts and closed end funds is exactly that. Often, and for various reasons such as outperformance of the trust, the impact of an effective share buy-back program and investor demand for trust shares, the discount will narrow and sometimes become a premium where the trust share price is in excess to its net asset value. If you get a ride up in price due to a narrowing or closing of a discount, that‘s great. It's not so great if you find the premium you paid disappearing or discount widening. This is a major risk with investment trusts and closed end funds and a simple value investment rule for investment trusts is; just don't buy a trust when its price is at a premium or, don't buy when the premium is at an historic high or greatly above its competitor trusts (trusts with comparable investment strategies).

In the UK, there are very good websites such as Trustnet and magazines such as Money Observer which cover the whole trust sector with detailed information and analysis. There is also and industry body for the investment trust sector that provides lots of basic information on its members.

There are few closed end funds in the US. There are also websites and analysts that specifically cover the closed end fund sector (commonly known as "CEFs). CEFs were much more common in the 19th and early 20th centuries. Exactly why the mutual fund industry overtook the closed end fund sector I do not know.

Of the websites that cover the US closed end fund sector one of is "CLEF" which provides very useful information on the various closed end funds.

Exchange Traded Funds (ETFs)

ETFs have been developed as a cost-effective alternative to mutual funds and unit trusts. They are exactly what they say they are: fund-type investments which are traded on a stock exchange, bought and sold through your broker at standard commission fees.

Some ETFs are passive; they track an established index such as the Dow Jones Industrial Average. Some ETFs create a "bundle" of sector-specific shares, usually using some kind of sector weighting (that is, buying shares of industry participants based on their market capitalization, for example, or using some other allocation formula such as equal weighting).

Some ETFs are actively managed, with a manager making share selections based on their own investment strategy.

In addition to ETFs there are ETCs (Exchange Traded Commodities and ETNs (Exchange Traded Notes). ETCs are ETFs that invest in specific commodities such as gold or coffee or sugar. ETNs are ETFs structured as debt notes. There are some very important differences worth noting.

There are physical ETFs and synthetic ETFs: a physical ETF invests in actual company shares, actual physical commodities such as bars of gold or tonnes of coffee or commodity futures contracts traded on commodity exchanges.

Synthetic ETFs use derivative instruments such as swaps to replicate the movement of their target investment. Synthetics have been developed to cope with situations where it is difficult or even impossible to buy the underlying real commodity or index or it's very difficult, inefficient or costly.

Synthetics are problematic and probably should be largely avoided. Here are the issues:

- Synthetics involve credit risks such as the counterparties to over-the-counter (OTC) derivative trades and OTC swaps (with counterparties such as banks).
- Synthetics often have very large tracking errors and hence don't replicate the performance of the underlying stock, index or commodity.
- Many synthetic ETFs are the type of ETF that tries to leverage the upside or downside movement of a stock, index or commodity. These are the types of ETFs that are meant to go up or down at twice or three times the underlying stocks, index or commodity. It has been repeatedly demonstrated that because of the techniques used and the behavior of derivatives markets, these types of ETFs, while interesting, only accurately track their underlying investments for short periods of time, i.e. days or a week. Over longer periods, i.e. a couple of weeks, they produce large and often contrary tracking errors (the commodity goes up in price and the ETF goes down).

For most investors, including us, the best strategy when using ETFs is to use unleveraged, physical ETFs. Using ETCs really depends on how comfortable you are with taking concentrated positions in certain commodities. Beyond some tracking problems, there is the simple issue of: are you a coffee trader? A wheat trader? On what basis and using what analytical tools and information are you going to select the commodity ETC?

ETFs are similar closed end funds. But they can and do issue shares to meet demand and they redeem or retire shares when demand declines. A good example of this has been the experience of gold bullion ETFs like the 'GLD', probably the largest gold bullion ETF in the US.

As the price of gold was rising steadily and dramatically from 2001 to 2013 this ETF and other gold ETFs issued additional shares to meet investor demand. This was done in part to keep the ETF trading at about par with the amount of gold bullion held by the ETF. The point was to avoid the ETF trading at a very large premium to gold prices. The point of the ETF was to be a convenient, low cost and very liquid way to "own gold" (own it indirectly). To do this effectively, the price of each ETF share has to correspond to the amount of gold held by the ETF, otherwise the investor isn't investing in gold, he's investing in the fund as if it were a company in its own right, which it is not and which is not the purpose the investment.

Criteria for choosing an instrument

Having given a brief overview of the types of investment instruments we can use in executing our investment plan, let's sum up the criteria we would use in choosing the instruments.

Risk Management

Depending upon an investor's particular attitude to risk the investor will want to factor in the following issues:

- Basic Risk Management – does the investment choice provide me with the risk characteristics I want (literally: high, medium or low)? Synthetic structures, leveraged structures, sector-specific funds present more risk.
- Diversification – does the investment choice provide me with a level of diversification of diversification I want?
- Comfort level and understanding – am I comfortable with the estimated risk: reward trade off provided by my choice and very importantly, do I understand what I'm getting into? If I don't, it's best avoided.

Market view and strategy

Investment choices should not be random or the "last best idea" you heard. They need to be congruent with your market outlook and your goals. Some great investors will say they never try to guess the direction of the market and some hedge fund investors stress that their views are "market neutral". They organize their portfolio to try to perform well regardless of the market's drift. But they always build their portfolios to meet their goals and their investment philosophy.

These considerations may seem blindingly obvious – but if they were so blindingly obvious the average investor would do a lot better over time than studies demonstrate we do. Investment management of your own capital requires discipline and requires that you apply that discipline systematically and consistently.

The reality is that lots of bright people, lots of professionally very successful people, treat their investment choices as if they were standing over a roulette table bemused by the choices presented. Stock market lore says that doctors and dentists are notorious for making "crazy" investment decisions and falling prey to private investment cons. To the extent that this is true, it's clear that in making investment choices these investors just don't apply the same processes they apply in dealing with our ailments and their own careers.

Summary

Remember:

1 "Collective investment schemes" – mutual funds, investment trusts and ETFs give us the benefit of professional management and monitoring. But we do want to and have to do research to determine which of those collective investment choices provides the best option for us in terms of meeting our risk and reward parameters. Professional management can be a great benefit and can be a choice we may want to make for part of our total portfolio.

2 ETFs are very good way to help us obtain diversification across sectors and geographic markets. We can feel

strongly about the Indian stock market but be at a loss on how to invest and what stocks to pick. An ETF can solve this problem very handily. ETFs have lower management fees than funds and they are liquid and can be traded easily through your broker.

3 Mutual funds can do much the same for you as ETFs but they're not as liquid; in a crisis they can defer redemption (repurchasing your shares) and they can have big up-front fees and fees levied if you try to sell your fund within the first 90 or 180 days after purchase (a redemption fee that can amount to 1% or more of the amount of your investment).

4 For UK investors, it's worth noting that there are unit trusts and investment trusts run by the same fund company, the same managers with the same strategy; they parallel each other and often the investment trust outperforms its "brother unit trust". Why? Sometimes it's down to lower management fees, sometimes to the movement of the investment trust from a discount to net assets to a premium. Sometimes it's the absence of a bid and offer spread (the investment fee charged buy the unit trust) and sometimes it's because it is easier for the managers to manage the investment trust portfolio than unit trust portfolio because they don't have to hold cash for daily redemptions and they don't have to manage the whole process of redeeming and accepting units and the inefficiency this creates in actually deploying the cash into investments.

Remember, it's the fund that sells and buys the units, so it has to keep a cash reserve which tends to earn very low returns because the cash reserve has to be liquid to meet daily redemptions. It also has to invest as chunks of money flow into the fund even in adverse market conditions if it is determined or by charter has to maintain a high minimum equity investment level.

Investment trusts and US closed end funds don't have to do any of this. They don't have to invest when they don't think it wise and they don't have to disinvest to meet investor redemptions.

Also investment trusts and closed end funds can borrow money to invest in their portfolio. To the extent that either the dividend yield or the total return on those investments is greater than the interest rate they have to pay, they are increasing their net asset value and their net return to the benefit of their shareholders.

Both trusts and closed end funds can also do share buybacks using excess cash (cash they don't feel comfortable investing) or borrowings to buy back their shares in the market with the intent of increasing the net asset value of the fund and hence its share price (as companies in terms of their legal structure they can do just what Microsoft does in this respect).

I really like investment trusts and ETFs; the best reason I can give for this is that I've been an active and so far happy investor in the health care and biotech trusts and ETFs. I know these are dynamic sectors with demographically driven growth prospects. I also know they are "specialist subjects". I like the "industry" but I don't have the ability to analyse and rank the participants. You need expertise in these areas well beyond any understanding I have or ever will have. And most often it's not a question of financial analysis – it's a matter of medical and medical industry, biochemistry and biotech industry expertise that counts. Specialist trusts and ETFs solve the problem of liking a sector but being unable to or uncomfortable with stock picking in that sector.

A word on fund fees: In the US and the UK funds and ETFs charge a wide range of management fees and performance related fees. The point to take into consideration is that over the long haul a difference of even one quarter of a per cent in comparative fund fee levels can make a meaningful difference in an investor's return experience.

The reason for this is "compounding". The compounding of a fee of say 1.25% over say 10 to 20 plus years really erodes the investor's ultimate return and this is particularly onerous if you stick with funds over the long term that are mediocre performers or under-perform their benchmark index.

One of the most common "tips" that market advisors give to private investors is "don't overpay" in terms of the management fees your fund charges. It is a valid point because inevitably many funds, over time, do not out-perform their benchmarks consistently.

Chapter 8

Technical Analysis

There are two schools of stock market analysis: Fundamental and Technical.

Fundamental Analysis is the most common and most well understood by investors. It involves analyzing companies, sectors or the market as a whole using a number of standard metrics such as price: earnings; price: cash flow; revenue growth trends; gross margin and gross profits trends; price: book value, and so on. Fundamental Analysis also places great emphasis on income statement, balance sheet and cash flow analysis.

Technical Analysis and its principal tool, Chart Analysis or Charting, involves analyzing stocks and the market by looking at stock price trends and patterns; the volume of stock traded; historical highs and lows not only for prices but also for price: earnings ratios, and many of the other measures and metrics used to evaluate individual stocks and markets as a whole.

Fundamental vs. Technical Analysis

Generally speaking, Fundamental Analysis proponents are dubious about Technical Analysts and Chartists and vice versa. Why?

Fundamentalists believe that much of Technical Analysis and all of Charting is nonsense and only by looking at the standard drivers of corporate performance and carefully reviewing and dissecting their financial reports can sensible, usable judgments about a company's prospects be made.

Technicians and Chartists believe that analyzing company financial statements is a largely a waste of time because:

- Companies lie and distort their income statements and balance sheets to present the most favorable picture of their affairs;
- Even when companies don't lie, the rules of accounting are so complicated and so seemingly twisted away from basic reality (just have a try at interpreting the notes to company's financial statements some time) that they obscure the facts of company performance and defeat the ability to make useful judgments.
- Furthermore, history shows repeatedly that good companies often don't match their share price trends to their operating and financial performance. Lots of really terrible companies (e.g. the internet disasters of the end of the "last century") experienced incredible share price appreciation while being nothing but "empty vessels" in terms of business models and actual performance. The opposite is also true, good companies generating cash and performing well can go on for years without matching share price gains. Why? Technical analysts will simply tell you it's all about supply and demand – the demand by investors for the company's shares which is driven by investor sentiment in the main.

Who's right? Both sides are. Investing is not a science with immutable laws hence is not surprising that fundamental tools work well in some instances and technical analysis in others.

But what's useful for us is to combine elements of both types of analysis. Technical Analysis and Chart Analysis can be very useful tools to help us sort out conflicting views about specific stocks or the market as a whole by giving us extra evidential information. They also have another important quality that I want to discuss.

Chart Analysis

Charting share price movements and using an array of tools to interpret those movements (the Technical Analysis tools) is based on the following key premises:

1. Shares prices, their trends and other metrics such as trading volumes are objective evidence of the attitudes of investors as a whole demonstrated through their buying and selling behavior. There's nothing subjective in this; Charting shows us in graphic form what investors are really up to, where they are putting in or removing their money.

2. Stock market activity is driven by its participants – human beings. The market just reflects the behavior of investors in aggregate. Stock markets and the behavior of stock prices are subject to the same behavioral characteristics as people. As such, there's no better way of interpreting the market than to be able to review what investors are doing – not saying, but doing – because, as opinion pollsters know, we lie or we delude ourselves when polled for our opinions. Actions speak louder than words.

The study of Behavioral Finance interprets economic activity and investing in terms of the psychology of human behavior. Again, Behavioral Finance, like Technical Analysis and Charting in particular, is based on the simple idea that markets are just "arenas" for human behavior in all its complexity and eccentricity.

Any investor familiar with Charting knows that Chartists can get carried away and in defense of Fundamental Analysis proponents, a lot of charting interpretation does sound like black magic. Additionally, and at least for the less visually oriented among us, many, many chart patterns are really difficult to discern because they're really vague in appearance thus giving scope to highly subjective interpretations.

We can avoid all that just by using charts and some basic Technical Analysis tools to help us sort out our views on a stock or the market and to evaluate how much credence we want to give to the views we read through our research.

The best way to explain how we can do this is just to look at a stock chart. There are many charting services on the Internet. Your broker's website will include a chart function. The quality of the charts and the ability of the users to manipulate them vary from site to site. In the UK, a very good charting function is available on the Investors Chronicle website. In the US, BigCharts.com is excellent and so is MSNMoney.com.

Many charting services have tutorials explaining their functionality and glossaries defining the various Technical Analysis` tools.

Let's take a look at the chart set out below. It's from BigCharts.com and it is a 6-month chart for an ETF called 'SCIF' which tracks India's Small-Cap Index.

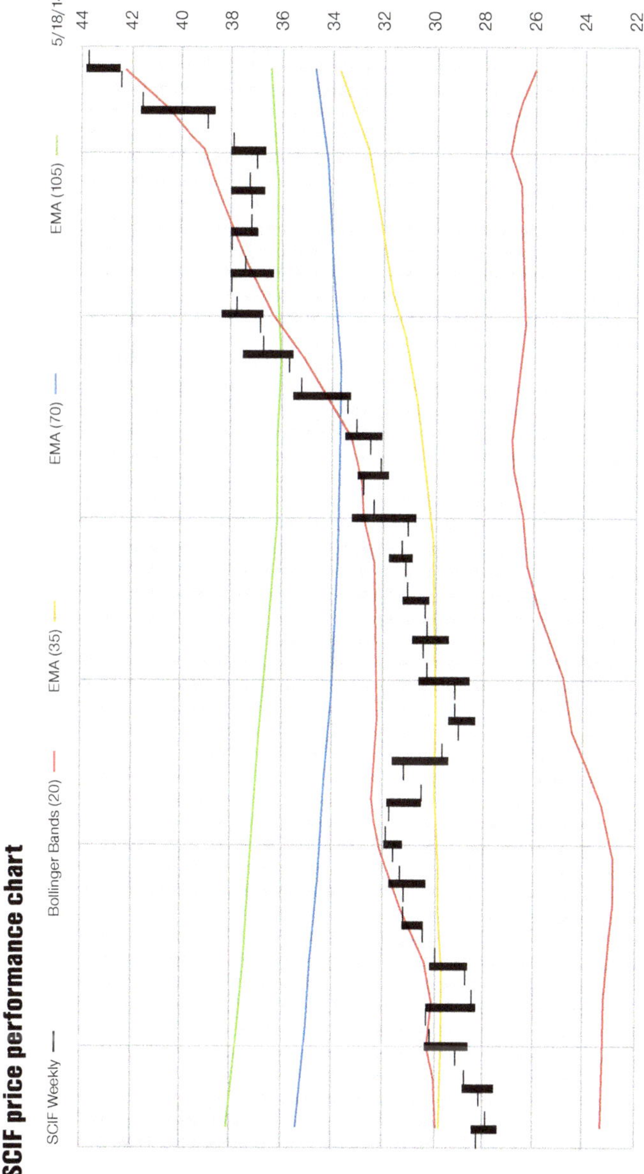

Chart courtesy of BigCharts

Looking across the top of the chart you can see both the then current (May 20, 2014) and historic information about the ETF. You can also see a Help function that includes a glossary. It's also worth noting that UK listed stocks can also be charted simply by tying in: UK: and then the epic code for that UK stock.

Down the right side of the chart is a list of drop-down menus for accessing both chart display characteristics, but also an array of Technical Analysis tools.

I have chosen a timeframe for the chart of 6 months and a frequency option of "weekly". My choices:

- I'm generally interested in viewing nearer term performance, the last 6 months, the last 3 months and sometimes the last month. If I'm trying to project out nearer term prices, I want to see the current momentum the stock has
- I choose weekly because I'm not day trading, not short-term trading and I don't want a lot of "noise", a lot of data I can't even absorb. Sure, there can be some big inter-week changes in share prices and we can set an option for a view using daily frequency, but normally a weekly time frame serves me well.

The "Compare To" function allows us to overlay our chosen stock or index with another stock or index for comparative purposes. We'll look at this function a bit later.

"Indicators" are our Technical Analysis tools and there are many to choose from. All of these tools are defined in the glossary, and if the definitions are not adequate, try Investopedia.com for more fulsome definitions and examples.

With benefit of experience, I use a couple of tools.

Bollinger Bands

Let's look at Bollinger Bands first. They are the two heavier red lines, the very top line and the very bottom line. Together, they are an historic volatility measure for SCIF's stock price. The gap between the two lines gives you a measure of how far up and how far down the stock might go, going forward.

Bollinger Bands are not boundaries, they're just a statistical measure of possible fluctuation and can easily be violated by the stock on the upside or downside. But they give a good graphic depiction of a stock's recent historic volatility.

A Bollinger Band rule of thumb: when a stock, like SCIF, is pushing the upper boundary there is a tendency for the price to then retreat. The obverse is also true; if a stock is touching its lower Bollinger Band there is a probability it will subsequently rise.

Moving averages

Moving averages measure the average stock price, based on closing prices, over any time period you choose (or the various time periods available on the site). I choose three time periods, 35 days, 70 days and 105 days. The way BigCharts operates is you choose your base period, 35 days in this case, and if you want 2 or 3 time periods the site just multiplies your base choice by 2 or 3.

I chose a short period, an intermediate and a longer-term period to give me a more balanced view of the stock's performance and performance characteristics. I chose an Exponential Moving Average rather a Simple Moving Average. In calculating the average an EMA gives greater weight to more recent periods. An SMA gives equal weight to all the time periods.

Why an EMA? Because I want to see the momentum, if any, in the stock; I want statistical emphasis on the stock's more recent prices.

Each EMA period is represented by a colored line. When the stock price moves above a line, that's positive momentum; when it drops below a line, that's negative momentum. I want positive momentum, a positive price trend.

Now, let's look at some more the tools shown.

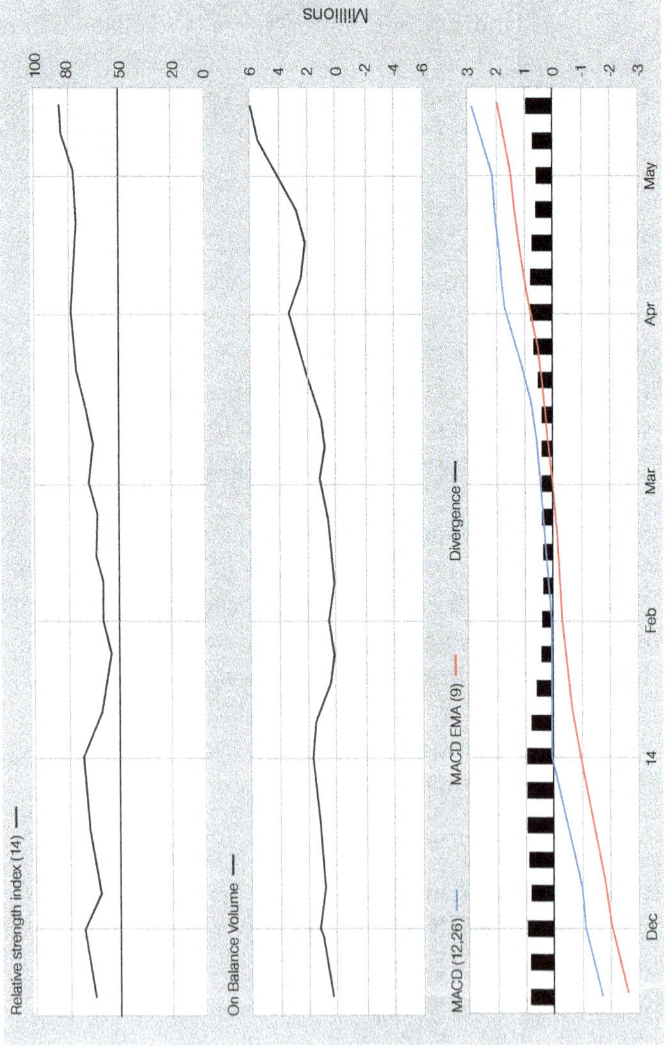

Chart courtesy of BigCharts

Relative Strength

The first analytical tool is Relative Strength. The RS Index measures the size of recent price rises to the size of recent price declines for a chosen stock, fund or ETF. It is a momentum indicator and is designed to try to help identify the stronger stocks in a market, those stocks with the strongest upward momentum.

It is generally considered that when the RSI is around the 70 mark or greater, it is "overbought" – meaning it has risen too far with too much investor enthusiasm and is likely to decline. Readings of around 20 or 30 have the opposite interpretation: the stock is "oversold".

The RSI can give lots of false signals. That's very important for traders who may try to use the RSI reading as signal for buying and selling points for a stock. For us, as investors, it's much less important. We're just using it as a measure of momentum. Largely speaking, I don't want to buy a stock with a very high RSI reading or a very low RSI reading. The RSI is a bit of "leading indicator" of what might happen in the nearer-term future and is useful as such.

On Balance Volume

This tool measures the relationship between trading volume (number of shares changing hands) on up-days and down-days. It's a measure of investor opinion about a stock. Investors vote with their money and if more shares are bought on days with price rises then are sold on down-days, the market is indicating a belief in still higher prices to come.

Additionally, if a technical analyst sees the OBV line rising and rising on modest volume, some analysts interpret this action as a sign that the smart money (e.g. institutional money) is buying the stock ahead of the broader market of individual investors. How accurate this interpretation of events may be is a matter of debate. But the basic interpretation and evidence is what I'm interested in.

Moving Average Convergence Divergence indicator

Lastly, I like to look at the so-called Moving Average Convergence Divergence indicator. The MACD measures the difference in direction between a short-term moving average and longer-term moving average. In this case, a 12-day and a 26-day moving average.

When those bars are above zero and when they are rising, it means that both averages are moving in the same direction – upwards. This is a pretty good positive momentum signal. When the bars are flat, getting flatter or are below zero and growing downwards, that's a very good negative signal for price expectation.

When the two averages are diverging and the bars are low or declining but above zero, that's a good indicator that the stock's price is very likely to be weak or negative going forward. What is being measured here are two time based price trends and when they contradict each other that is an indicator of a possible change in the direction of the price.

When I want to get a better feel for any stock or ETF that I've read about and that has been recommended by an equity magazine or newsletter, I like to look at its chart configured as I have done above. I often alter the time periods and frequencies if I want a closer look or have some doubts about what I'm first seeing and am having trouble forming an investment decision, a buy or a sell out of position I'm no longer happy with.

The Display / Chart appearance functions

Here you choose what's best for you. What's easiest on the eye, what appeals to you, what makes it easier to read the chart. There are various ways to display the stock price, including bar charts, mountains, the traditional open-high-low-close stick figure I used and others. I want the one that has the least "noise", the easiest for me to see and read. Sometimes I use bars, sometimes the mountain. A lot depends on what you're trying to see. If you want to see the moving average lines then the o-h-l-c stick figure is just better for visual reasons.

I am not a really visual person so I don't look for all sorts of exotic, arcane chart patterns. Reading chartists' analysis of arcane patterns is really boring and off-putting for me. I use simply constructed charts and what are for me reasonably well-understood technical tools to try to confirm Fundamental Analysis opinions of stocks.

I really like the concept that charts and the tech tools show you real money investment action, real investor behavior and give you a basis for making some projections of price using the Technical Analysis tools.

Technical Analysis and charts are a great way for me to deal with uncertainty and ambiguity that is central to stock markets and investor behavior.

Using the Compare function on charts

Depending on charting program you're using, you can create charts comparing your "base" stock or fund selection to one or more indices or other stocks and funds.

The visual quality of the output varies from charting site to site due to the differing graphical styles the sites use and some sites are visually better than others. The quality of the underlying information is the same.

The Compare function is a very good visual method for analyzing and making choices between or among investment options after you have done some numerical analysis. For the Compare function to be of genuine use, you have to be comparing "apples with apples".

The key "apple" is the risk profile of the options you're comparing. Each option has to be within your designated risk profile – that is your essential base position for capital conservation and Risk Management.

You can and will invest in higher risk, growth oriented stocks but there is no real logic to comparing a conservative, income stock to a growth stock. They are not equivalent alternatives. You will have satellite portfolios for various investment styles such as income and growth and income stocks will go into your income satellite portfolio and growth into your growth portfolio and so on. You are not going to be making choices between one income stock versus one particular growth stock as the next investment you make. You could be making judgments between income and growth stocks in terms of the next category of stock you invest in.

Using the Compare function you are now trying to decide between similar investment options, the next addition you will make to a particular sub-portfolio.

Using a chart for analysis

Using MSN Money.com's charting program, which is very clear visually, I've created the following chart comparing Annaly Mortgage to two other mortgage REITs: New York Mortgage Trust (NYMT) and American Agency Capital (AGNC). All three REITs are essentially in the same business, all three are well run. Here's some basic information.

				52-week	
REIT	**Yield**	**Rating**	**Price**	**High**	**Low**
Annaly	10.26%	3.2 / 4.0	$11.67	$14.95	$9.66
AGNC	11.14%	3.2 / 4.0	$23.25	$29.49	$18.84
NYMT	10.28%	Not rated	$7.71	$5.55	$8.12

Dividend.com

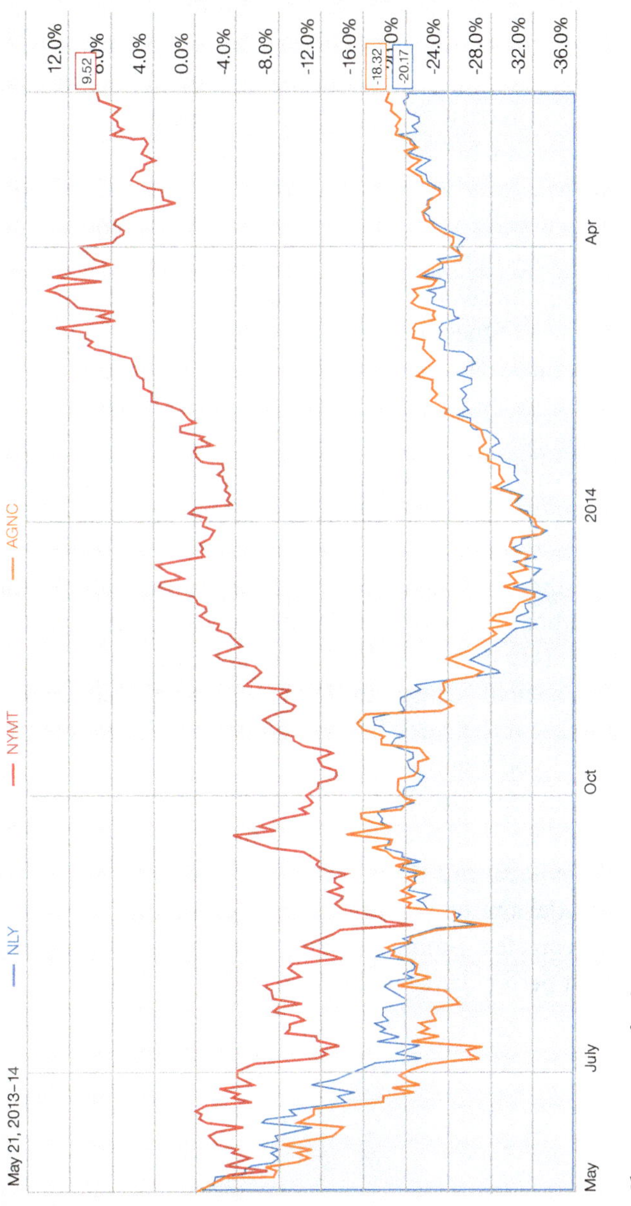

Chart courtesy of MSN Money.com

In our comparative chart, with Annaly as the base stock, we can see that NLY and AGNC's price performance over one year is virtually the same. Over the course of 52 weeks, NLY's price declined by 20.17% and AGNC's by 18.32%. In contrast, NYMT's price rose by 9.52% over the same period.

The reason for NLY and AGNC's price decline over the period was due to market concerns about Federal Reserve monetary policy: was QE (money printing and super low interest rates) going to continue, were interest rates going to rise precipitously hitting the demand for home finance (mortgages), would there be a rise in mortgage defaults due to rising interest rates? During the period under review, lots of income stocks were hurt significantly by interest rate and policy uncertainty.

Why did NYMT outperform so significantly? I don't really know and my research using the independent research reports available through Fidelity do not give me answer. They do tell me that NYMT has been cited as having both "corporate governance" risk and using "aggressive" accounting.

What is to be done? I have three options:

Take a small position in NYMT with a tight but appropriate stop to see if the stock has continuing upward momentum in relation to NLY and AGNC.

Pass and focus on NLY and AGNC on the basis that the past is, in this instance, not a reliable indicator of the future. I'll rely on the risk ratings these two REITs have received. The yield differential among the three is not meaningful.

I can create a 3-month chart to see what the recent and more relevant performance of the three REITs has been:

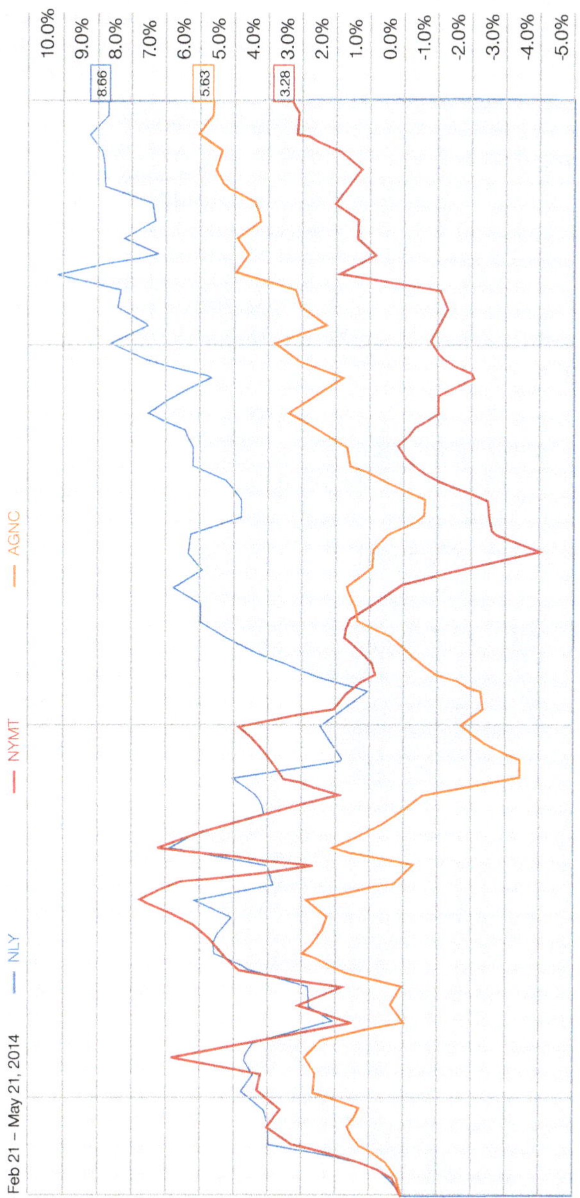

Chart courtesy of MSN Money.com

Now we see both NLY and AGNC significantly outperforming NYMT.

I must tell you that if I now create a 1-month chart we would see NYMT outperform NLY but somewhat underperform AGNC. Not a lot of certainty gained here.

Now, what to do?

I can put NYMT on a watch list and track it over the ensuing months to see how it performs and whether I might want to revise my opinion.

Most immediately I would pass on NYMT – unnecessary uncertainty. There is little difference in yield, and NLY and AGNC are widely followed and very liquid mortgage REITs and hence the uncertainty (in effect, the real notion of risk) is greatly lessened for me as an investor.

As you can see there's an element of investing that is just "not easy". If it were easy we'd all be John Templeton or Peter Lynch and there would little or no need for books like this.

Appendix 1

Stop Limits: A Trading Tactic for Dealing with Uncertainty

A trading or buying tactic that I use frequently when I am uncertain about a stock or the direction and tone of the market but am strongly contemplating the purchase of a particular investment is to use my broker's "Stop Limit" buying function on its drop-down "Buy" menu on the trading function page.

If I am prepared to buy a stock or ETF I'm interested in but have concerns about it, I may buy in *if the investment shows upward momentum in near term.* I can set a "Stop Limit Buy Order". In setting this type of order I set a "stop price" – a price at which I am happy to buy the stock, that stop price is above the current market price because I want to see upward momentum before I buy into the investment. The Limit Price is set above the Stop Price and is the highest price I am currently prepared to pay for the stock. The purpose of the Limit Price is that if the stock suddenly soared upward by say 3% –5% I don't want to buy into that level without further proof of sustainable momentum. I don't want to "buy high" and end up selling low if the stock backs off of some sudden, unsustainable, unsupported rise.

When setting a Stop Limit Buy Order I choose an order time frame greater than one day. Whatever time frame I set I do refer back to this type of "Open Order" to see what the stock price is in relation to the Stop Price level. If the stock has gone down in value I may just cancel the order. If the stock has zoomed past my buy and limit levels, I'll cancel. I can always adjust the buy and limit levels downward or upward if I have cause to do so.

Appendix 2

Conviction Investing

This term has become popular over the last decade. George Soros, the well-known trader, may have been the catalyst for the popularization of this style of investing.

As previously mentioned Conviction Investing or Trading simply consists of taking large to very large position in a limited number of individual investments, for example; taking positions on the order of 20% of your total portfolio value.

If you want to really outperform an index this is a way of doing it.

Without being unduly cynical, Conviction Investing is a great thing when investing "other people's money". It plays to the so-called "trader's option" (the option is; if the trader is right he gets a giant bonus, if wrong, he loses your money, not his!).

Lots of hedge funds regularly take Conviction positions but, there doing it with their investor's money and they're doing it in a context where they take big management fees with the "option" of picking up huge performance fees if they are "right".

It's debatable if Conviction Investing is at all appropriate for private investors investing their own money without any form of trader's option.

It's also worth noting in an overall portfolio context that most us do take Conviction positions; e.g. our jobs (particularly in an age of high job insecurity at all levels and in all industries – most jobs exclude the possibility of having a concurrent second job) and our housing. Those two positions may be all the conviction any investor should undertake.

Appendix 3

Rule 1, Stop Losses and Risk Management

How important is Rule 1 and the use of stop losses and other risk management tools? The simplest possible example: if you allow yourself to lose 50% on an investment, how much does the investment have to recover for you to break even? Well, of course, it's 100%. How many 100% return investments have you really? And that just gets to break-even.

Perhaps more realistically and tellingly, let's say you lose 25%, what do you have to recoup? About 33%: please note that really good professional investors are people who can consistently earn 10–15% annually. Fund managers who consistently earn their clients returns in this range are singled out as "stars". Consistency means a lot, but so does actually being able to just bank several 10–15% gains.

There are of course realized and unrealized losses. With an unrealized loss (you haven't sold your investment) you are waiting and hoping for a recovery in share price along the lines of the magnitudes set out above. Five years ago I urged an acquaintance to take their heavy losses in UK bank stocks and at least use the tax losses and reinvest the funds because to get back to break-even with Royal Bank of Scotland and Lloyds the acquaintance would have had to see literally 100% + gains. Five years on there has not been these almost impossible share price rises. Waiting and hoping is a psychological / behavioral investment phenomenon. It is a futile attempt to avoid the pain of loss and the impact this has on our self-esteem more.

With a realized loss we have to face the reality that we now have a diminished amount of capital to redeploy and with that diminished amount of capital is likely to come an enlarged fear of loss, an increased risk aversion. Fear kills traders and it can cripple investors. Unsurprisingly, it distorts our judgment and hence our ability to sensibly, efficiently and successfully deploy our capital.

A 100% gain! Here is some market information on achievable returns:

- Over the period 1900–2008, Credit Suisse estimated that the average annual return for the US stock market was 11.1% and for the world excluding the US, it was 9.7%.
- Looking at the period 2000 – end 2008 and including the 2007–2008 crash, Credit Suisse estimates the return from US large company stocks was minus 3.6% and for small company stocks 4.1% per annum.
- Last point: Do you remember the tech bust of 1999–2001? There are private investors who had not recovered their lost capital from this crash even as of 2015 and they were not helped by the crash of 2007–2008.

I think by now you've gotten the message as to why you don't want to run double-digit losses on a regular basis.

Appendix 4

Inflation and the Battle for Investment Survival

Inflation is an insidious enemy. Part of the battle for conservation of capital is avoiding losses from bad investments but another constant, continuing battle is against inflation.

Simply stated: the US and the UK governments consider 2% price inflation to be acceptable over the long term. That target is, as many of you know, rarely met. But for argument's sake, let's use 2%. Say you determine today, *at today's prices,* that it would be great to retire with a capital amount saved of $500,000. With this amount you'll have the second home and the boat you've always dreamed of. You've got 30 years to go to retirement. Want to know what $500,000 will have for purchasing power in 30 years at 2% inflation? The answer is $276,000 – goodbye house and boat! And that's a very "modest" rate of inflation.

We've had higher than 2% inflation in both the US and UK earlier this century. Now thanks to QE and deflation we have sub 1% inflation but with Quantitative Easing we're likely to have double-digit inflation over the next decade as all that artificial money washes eventually through the economy. Maybe that won't happen because as many analysts and economists argue we are locked in a long-term deflationary cycle. In any event *reversion to the mean* and 2% plus inflation is likely to occur at some point in the not too distant future.

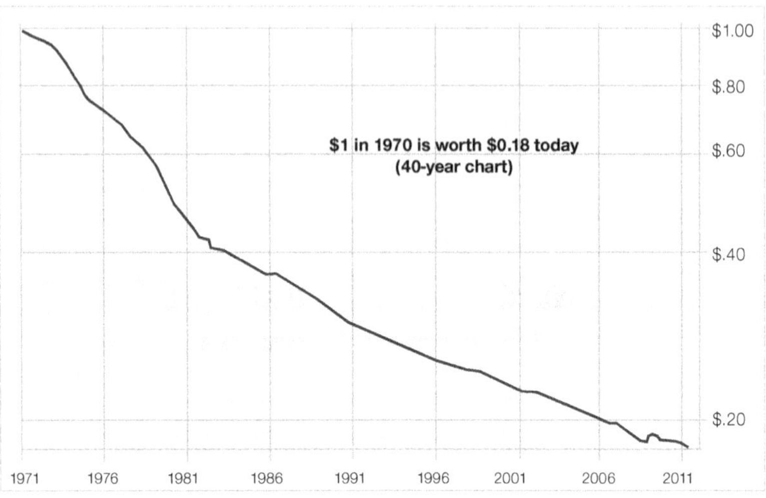

Why is inflation so bad

Inflation poses a serious risk, as it erodes both the capital value of investments and the income from them. When assessing the returns from an investment it is important to consider the 'real' return. If an investment grows by 5% during a year, but at the end of that year goods and services have become 5% more expensive, the real return is zero.

In the 1970s, inflation ran at an average of 13% (reaching a horrifying 25% in 1975). Today's inflation looks low by comparison, but defending capital and the spending power of returns should be a priority for investors.

Inflation hits lower returns disproportionately hard. Over the past 40 years (1971 to 2010) the stock market has delivered average returns of 12.0% a year, while cash managed 7.3% – great compared to today's low interest rate. However, after taking inflation into account, equities' average annual return was cut by just over half to 5.3%. But cash returns were much harder hit, falling to just 1.0%.

Of course, cash remains a very important safety net, and all investors maintain a cash reserve to cover emargencies and unforseen circumstances. However, with interest rates seemingly aet to stay relatively low and inflation running at 4%, cash is losing its value in real terms, so many invetsors need to consider taking some risk to maintain and grow their wealth.

How inflation erodes your buying power

What £1,000 will be worth in real terms...

Rate of Inflation	2.5%	5.0%	7.5%	10.0%
In 5 years	£884	£784	£697	£621
In 10 years	£781	£614	£485	£386
In 15 years	£690	£481	£338	£239
In 20 years	£610	£377	£235	£149
In 30 years	£477	£231	£114	£57
In 40 years	£372	£142	£55	£22

Quantitative easing explained

With the conventional weaponry of lowering interest rates exhausted, central banks in the US and UK have resorted to QE to rejuvenate their economies.

What is QE?

QE is Plan B. It refers to a central bank's attempt to inject more money into the economy, by purchasing privately held assets such as government or corporate bonds with newly created money.

How is it supposed to work?

This extra money is supposed to boost spending and growth in three ways. Firstly, it should help bring down borrowing costs, making it easier for companies to invest and households to spend. Secondly, if the money is used to buy other assets such as shares, rising stock markets should also lift household wealth and thus spending. Thirdly, the side-effect of a weakened currency should pave the way for a stronger exports performance.

Appendix 5

Correlation and Diversification

I want to show you a really interesting phenomenon; gold vs. gold mining stocks.

You would assume that gold bullion prices and gold mining stocks would be highly correlated, which they largely are. But the relationship between the relative values of an index of gold miners and the gold bullion price is not stable (this is also true for other commodities and their producers).

Look at the chart below that compares the prices for the GLD gold ETF and the GDX gold miners ETF over 5 years. You can clearly see how the relationship / ratio between the two indices widen and narrows over time.

This means that if you were to choose gold as the investment vehicle for the Theme of the devaluation of fiat / paper money you would have had very different returns depending on whether you chose gold or gold miners as your investment or by varying your allocation of investment capital over both assets.

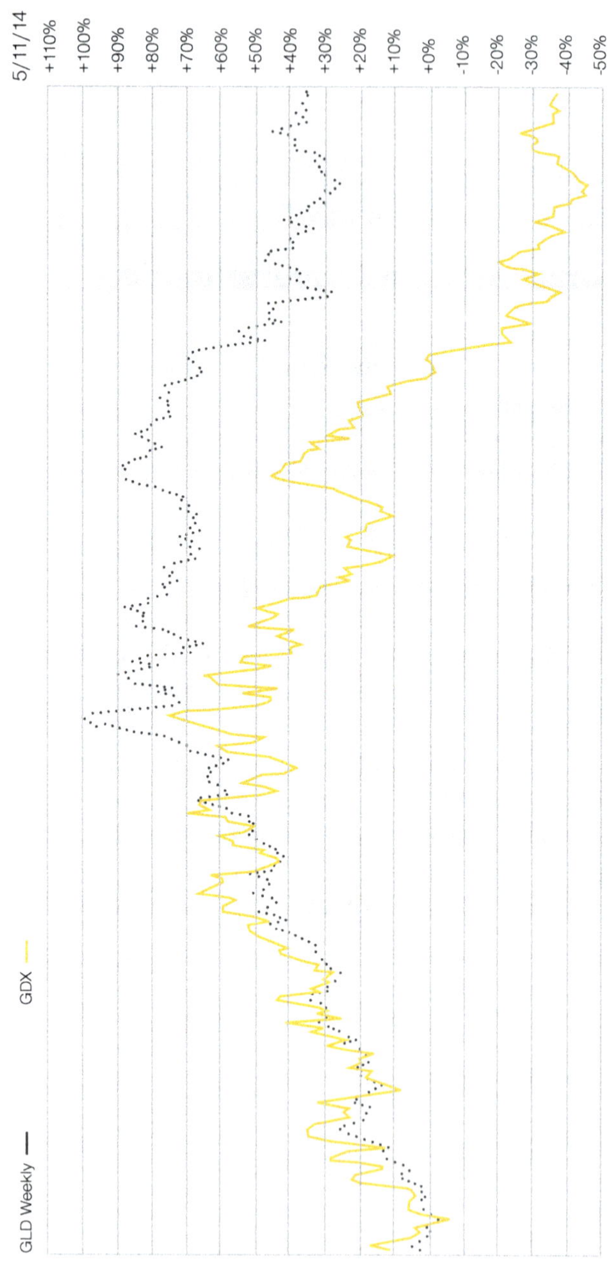
5/11/14
+110%
+100%
+90%
+80%
+70%
+60%
+50%
+40%
+30%
+20%
+10%
+0%
-10%
-20%
-30%
-40%
-50%
GLD Weekly
GDX

In the chart above the dots represent the Gold Bullion ETF (GLD) monthly over a 5-year period. The line is the Gold Mining ETF (GDX). You can see that, while the movement of the two ETFs track each other, their relative performance is hugely different.

Appendix 6

Modern Portfolio Theory

Yes, there is a thing called Modern Portfolio Theory, which emphasizes a principle called the Efficient Investment Frontier. The Efficient Investment Frontier is a point on a graphed curve where the investor can achieve the maximum return for a stated degree of risk.

This is very elegant piece of theory and it makes for nice graphic representation. Unlike lots of other economic and financial market theories however it's not only pragmatic but also, the tools for implementing the concept are actually readily available.

The Efficient Investment Frontier

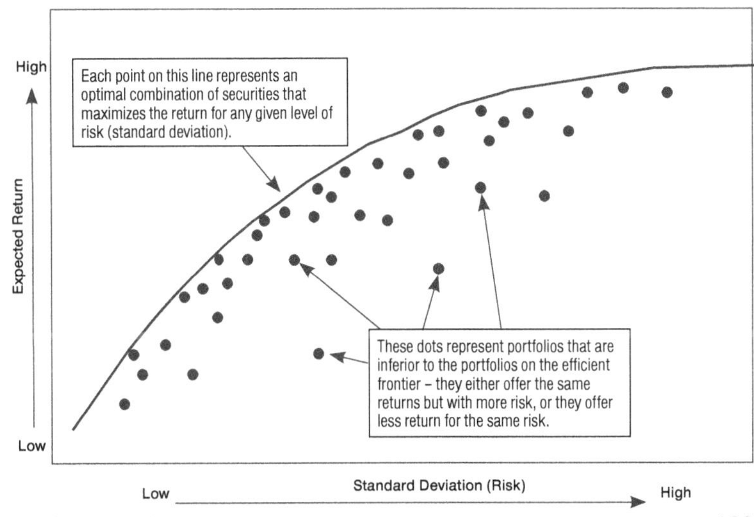
High
Each point on this line represents an optimal combination of securities that maximizes the return for any given level of risk (standard deviation).
Expected Return
These dots represent portfolios that are inferior to the portfolios on the efficient frontier – they either offer the same returns but with more risk, or they offer less return for the same risk.
Low
Low
Standard Deviation (Risk)
High

Source: Investing Answers

This is an example of an Efficient Frontier graph. The vertical axis is the expected return of any given stock or portfolio of stocks, the horizontal axis is risk as measured by Standard Deviation of Risk. As you would expect, the lower the risk of an asset, the lower its "acceptable" (efficient return) is.

What is *Efficient*? It's the return that matches the expected degree of risk. If the return is too low for the risk then it's not "efficient". As with any similarly constructed graph, the dot has to be located at the highest point on the graph to qualify as being "a best choice" or a "best performer" or whatever the graph is meant to measure or illustrate. The dot is the intersection of that stock's risk and reward. Every dot is a stock or a combination of stocks or a combination of assets or whatever you want to look at. The Efficient Frontier Line is just the line that connects most of the highest situated dots.

Appendix 7

Top Down or Bottom Up?

With reference to portfolio construction and investment selection I want to discuss two common approaches to investment analysis and share selection, Top Down and Bottom Up.

Equity analysts, investors and investment managers often differentiate themselves according to which of these analytical processes they follow. What do these terms mean? What is the relevance for us?

Both approaches are based on a need to rationalize the equity investment effort. As you know, there is a myriad of share choices in the market and if we invest across geographic boundaries, the range of possible equity investment choices becomes that much wider.

Not surprisingly, many analysts and investors feel the need to impose a "search discipline" in order to work efficiently and with a logical consistency. Furthermore, there is a philosophical difference. Top Down analysts and investors believe the most effective investment process is to:

1 **First, decide on asset allocation issues:** that is, choosing between or among equities, fixed income, property or even somewhat more "exotic" assets such as stamps, coins, art or physical precious metals (i.e. gold and silver bars). Not all analysts start here because some analysts and investors are wholly focused only on equities, for example.

2 **Second, decide on market focus and allocation:** this is relevant if you invest across geographic markets.

3 **Third, decide on market sectors:** this is a step common to all Top Down investors. A review of macro-economic, political and socio-economic factors and trends leads to a decision on which sectors or industries the investor wants to be in. It also can influence choice of investment style. By style we mean choosing among an emphasis on growth or value or defensive sectors depending on market outlook and investor risk preferences.

4 **Fourth, decide on individual stocks:** by virtue of the all the analysis and decisions taken in steps 1 through 3, the investor can now make consistent, logical individual investment choices. Note that the investor doesn't have to drill down to the individual stock level. He or she can stop at the sector level and choose among the various mutual funds or ETFs that cover the sector, either passively or actively.

Bottom Up analysts and investors take the opposite approach, as the phrase suggests.

Bottom Up investors believe that stock picking is the critical factor for investment success and moreover, most such investors would define investment success as "outperforming the market" – outperformance of some benchmark index of their choosing.

Bottom Up investors necessarily believe that they have the ability to identify specific stocks that will outperform over some investment horizon. It's fair to say that in general Top Down investors and analysts do not share this belief, both in terms of their own ability to identify "winning" stocks from the entire equity investment universe or any investor's ability to do this on a consistent basis and that is why they follow a structured Top Down methodology.

It's probably correct that in principle the real outperformance of any market benchmark (the Dow, the FTSE 100, etc.) can only be achieved through stock picking. Think of this in terms of a roulette table – to really hit it big during a session of roulette gambling you will need to bet on single numbers where the odds are steepest but the reward is the highest.

Now, roulette is a complete non-skill game as far as I can determine. Stock picking, to continue the gambling metaphor, is more like playing Black Jack (Twenty-One). But again, as with roulette, you're going to have to be aggressive, in this instance, splitting and doubling-down if you want to outperform.

Bottom Up analysts and investors follow a variety of methods using a range of stock valuation metrics to make their investment selections. The ability to manage the Bottom Up approach is now widely available to all investors including you and me. Many equity websites and broker web platforms include the ability to screen stocks using a wide range of criteria as part of their market research offer.

Both approaches are completely valid and which one you choose really depends on your investment philosophy. In terms of Thematic Investing, I think you can understand that we logically work from a Top Down approach since we are looking to identify and invest into key economic, political and social trends.

We will use stock screens because, having identified a Theme that leads us to a market sector we then want to try to make the best specific investment choices we can from that sector. Even in a clearly strong market sector there has to be better quality stocks and lower quality stocks (although I dislike the phraseology, "there will be winners and losers"). We can, as mentioned above, focus the search at the higher level of sector funds rather than do the drilling-down effort to identify particular stocks.

Appendix 8

Position Sizing – an Essential Element of Trading Success

The following is an excerpt from an Internet financial newsletter called the *Daily Wealth Trader* that I think you may find very useful.

The Daily Crux: Brian, one of the most important things any new investor can learn is correct position sizing. Can you define the idea for us?

Brian Hunt: Sure... Position sizing is an incredibly important part of your investment or trading strategy. If you don't know the basics of this concept, it's unlikely you'll ever succeed in the market. Fortunately, it's an easy concept to grasp.

Position sizing is the part of your investment or trading strategy that tells you how much money to place into a given trade.

For example, suppose an investor has a $100,000 account. If this investor buys $1,000 worth of shares in company ABC, his position size would be 1% of his total capital. If the investor bought $3,000 worth of stock, his position size is 3% of his total capital.

Many folks think of position size in terms of how many shares they own of a particular stock. But the successful investor thinks in terms of what percentage of their total account is in a particular stock.

Crux: Why is position sizing so important?

Hunt: Position sizing is the first and probably most important way investors can protect themselves from what's known as the "catastrophic loss".

The catastrophic loss is the kind of loss that erases a large chunk of your investment account. It's the kind of loss that ends careers... and even marriages.

The catastrophic loss typically occurs when a trader or investor takes a much larger position size than he should. He'll find a stock, commodity, or option trade he's really excited about, start dreaming of all the profits he could make, and then make a huge bet.

He'll place 20%, 30%, 40% or more of his account in that one idea. He'll "swing for the fences" and buy 2,000 shares of a stock instead of a more sensible 300 shares. He'll buy 20 option contracts when he should buy three.

The obvious damage from the catastrophic loss is financial. Maybe that investor who starts with $100,000 suffers a catastrophic 80% loss and is left with $20,000. It takes most folks years to make back that kind of money from their job.

But the less obvious damage is worse than losing money... It's the mental trauma that many people never recover from. They can get knocked out of investing forever. They just stick their money in the bank and stop trying. They consider themselves failures. They see years of hard work – as represented by the money they accumulated from their job or business – flushed down the toilet. It's a tough "life pill" to swallow. Their confidence gets shattered.

So clearly, you want to avoid the catastrophic loss at all costs... And your first line of defense is to size your positions correctly.

Crux: What are the guidelines for choosing a position size?

Hunt: Most great investors will tell you to never put more than 4% or 5% of your account into any one position. Some professionals won't put more than 3% in one position. 1%, which is a much lower risk per position, is better for most folks.

Seasoned investors may vary position size depending on the particular investment. For example, when buying a safe, cheap dividend stock, a position size of up to 5% may be suitable. Some managers who have done a ton of homework on an idea and believe the risk of a significant drop is nearly non-existent will even go as high as 10% or 20% – but that's more risk than the average investor should take on.

When dealing with more volatile vehicles – like speculating on junior resource stocks or trading options – position sizes should be much smaller... like a half a percent... or 1%.

Unfortunately, most novices will risk three, five, or 10 times as much as they should. It's a recipe for disaster if the company or commodity they own suffers a big, unforeseen move... or when the market in general suffers a big unforeseen move. These big, unforeseen moves happen with much greater frequency than most folks realize.

Crux: Can you explain how the math works with position sizing?

Hunt: Yes... But first I need to explain a concept that goes hand in hand with determining correct position sizing: protective stop losses.

A protective stop loss is a predetermined price at which you will exit a position if it moves against you. It's your "uncle" point where you say, "Well, I'm wrong about this one, time to cut my losses and move on."

Most people use stop losses that are a certain percentage of their purchase price. For example, if a trader purchases a stock at $10 per share, he could consider using a 10% stop loss. If the stock goes against him, he would exit the position at $9 per share... or 10% lower than his purchase price.

If that same trader uses a stop loss of 25%, he would sell his position if it declined to $7.50 per share, which is 25% less than $10.

Generally speaking, a stop loss of 5% is considered a "tight stop"– that is close to your purchase price – and a 50% stop loss is considered a "wide stop" – that is a long way from your purchase price.

Combining intelligent position sizing with stop losses will ensure the trader or investor a lifetime of success. To do this, we need to get familiar with the concept many people call "R."

Crux: Please explain...

Hunt: "R" is the value you will "risk" on any one given investment. It is the foundation of all your position-sizing strategies.

For example, let's return to the example of the investor with a $100,000 account. We'll call him Joe.

Joe believes company ABC is a great investment, and decides to buy it at $20 per share.

But how many shares should he buy? If he buys too many, he could suffer a catastrophic loss if an accounting scandal strikes the company. If he buys too little, he's not capitalizing on his great idea.

Here's where intelligent position sizing comes into play. Here's where the investor must calculate his R.

> R is calculated from two other numbers. One is total account size. In this case, it's $100,000. The other number is the percentage of the total account you'll risk on any given position.
>
> Let's say Joe decides to risk 1% of his $100,000 account on the position. In this case his R is $1,000. If he decided to dial-up his risk to 2% of his entire account, his R would be $2,000. If he was a novice or extremely conservative, he might go with 0.5%, or an R of $500.
>
> Joe is going to place a 25% protective stop loss on his ABC position. With these two pieces of information, he can now work backwards and determine how many shares he should buy.

Remember... Joe's R is $1,000, and he's using a 25% stop loss.

To calculate how large the position will be, the first step is to always divide 100 by his stop loss.

In Joe's case, 100 divided by 25 results in four. Now, he performs the next step in figuring his position size. He then takes that number – four – and multiplies it by his R of $1,000.

Four times $1,000 is $4,000, which means Joe can buy $4,000 worth of ABC stock... or 200 shares at $20 per share.

If ABC declines 25%, he'll lose $1,000 – 25% of his $4,000 – and exit the position.

That's it. That's all it takes to practice intelligent position sizing.

Here's the calculation again:

100 divided by your stop loss equals "A."

"A" multiplied by "R" equals position size.

Finally, position size divided by share price equals the number of shares to buy.

Now... what if Joe wants to use a tighter stop loss – say 10% – on his ABC position? Let's do the math...

100 divided by 10 equals 10.

10 multiplied by $1,000 equals $10,000.

$10,000 divided by the same $20 share price equals 500 shares.

So you can see that using a tighter stop loss with the same R allows Joe to buy a larger number of shares, while risking the same amount of his total account... $1,000.

> Next, let's say Joe wants to use a super-tight stop loss of just 5% on his position. In this case, if ABC declines just 5% to $19 per share, he's out of the trade.
>
> This tighter stop loss means he can buy even more shares. Let's do the math again...
>
> 100 divided by 5 equals 20.
>
> 20 multiplied by $1,000 equals $20,000.
>
> $20,000 divided by the $20 share price equals 1,000 shares.
>
> Again, a tighter stop loss with the same R of $1,000 means he can buy twice as many shares and still risk the same amount of his total account.

As you can see, you can use the concepts of position sizing and stop losses to determine how much of any asset to buy... from crude oil futures to currencies to microcaps to Microsoft.

If you're trading a riskier, more volatile asset, the stop loss percentage should typically increase and the position size should decrease.

If you're investing in a safer, less volatile asset, the stop loss percentage should decrease and the position size should increase.

And like I mentioned earlier, a good, "middle of the road" R that will work for anyone is 1% of your total account. Folks new to the trading game would be smart to start with half of 1% of their account. This way, you can be wrong 10 times in a row and lose just 5% of your account.

Crux: Any closing thoughts?

Hunt: Again, the biggest thing intelligent position sizing does is keep you from suffering the catastrophic loss. The golden rule of investing or trading is, "Don't lose money." Intelligent position sizing ensures you always follow rule number one.

Appendix 9

ETFs and hedge funds

I mentioned that there are various ways of hedging your equity exposure that allow you to maintain your long positions in the face of concerns about market-wide trends, industry or stock specific price trends or potential big events like a market collapse. Among the tools that can be used are Inverse ETFs. Inverse exchange traded funds are ETFs designed to rise in value as the underlying asset falls in value. This effect is accomplished in different ways depending on the ETF structure / mechanics chosen by its creator, the management company. The key points in brief:

- A perfect hedge would mean that you would never gain or lose on your positions. A perfect hedge is hard to achieve and unless your interest is to maintain your long position in order to collect dividends and forego any possible growth you wouldn't even want a perfect hedge if it could be achieved. (By the way, getting towards "perfection" is possible but cumbersome and technically complicated. The process is called "dynamic hedging" and what it involves is continuously reviewing and changing your hedge position based on the price change in the stock(s) you are trying to hedge and some other key dynamics such the prevailing rate of change of both the stock to be hedged and the hedge instrument itself.)

- What you largely want to do is to mitigate the impact of a "shock loss" of size or a "drift downward" in the price of your long position. After either the shock has occurred or the drift has seemingly ended, you will want to "unwind" the hedge. That is, you will keep the stock (your long position) and hence close out / sell your hedge security or vice versa, depending on your view what is likely to follow.
- Not all ETFs are equal (inverse or regular). Some inverse ETFs achieve the directional performance they aim for by shorting the actual stock or commodity they hedge. Others do so either by entering into swaps with counterparties such as banks or using derivatives. Market analysts and advisors will counsel that it is best to use those ETFs that actually short the stock from both a risk and performance perspective.

  The second best solution is those ETFs that use market traded futures and options, again for safety and performance reasons.

  The least desirable ETFs are those that use swap trades with banks. There are counterparty risk issues (e.g. the bank on the other side of the swap trade goes bankrupt – see Lehman Brothers). Additionally these swaps are not market listed and traded and are not liquid, and they may not perform in line with the movement of the underlying stock or commodity; hence the ETF and its investors will not get the performance they should have had / would have expected.

Hedge funds – the bleak reality

The point here is not just to debunk hedge funds or rail against their managers who have largely engorged and enriched themselves at the expense of their investors (I'll do this anyway) but to emphasize the point that lots of private investors can largely achieve better results than the average hedge fund without paying excessive fees, being locked into illiquid investments and being in thrall to puffed-up financial robber barons.

One reason a private investor can improve on average or industry-wide returns is that the term hedge fund, is a term of art. It has no legal or regulatory meaning in itself. There are literally tens of thousands of so-called hedge funds around the world. The vast majority of these entities have adopted the term hedge fund for marketing and status reasons and the use of the term in no way implies anything special about the strategies or techniques used by the fund manager. As a matter of fact a lot of these funds don't even "hedge" any of their positions and many are just long-only funds resembling in approach the "central tendency" of the mutual fund / unit trust industry to which they're supposed to be an alternative.

Are there are uniquely talented hedgies? Yes, there genuinely are. There are the John Paul Tudors, John Paulsons, Chris Hohns and a handful of others. Uniquely talented managers are not to be confused with simply the highest earning managers – high management earnings are not synonymous with high performance for their investors (see below). They are synonymous with fund size and the gall of the managers' fee-charging scheme and the commissions he's prepared to pay to entities that gather and channel investable money.

Research by a trio of US academics (Clifford, Aiken and Ellis) analysed the returns of thousands of hedge funds that are SEC-registered and hence presumably report performance reasonably honestly. There are a number of hedge fund databases such as the Credit Suisse Tremont Index among others (many of which you can access on the net for free (you get their basic performance data set)).

These databases are dependent on the voluntary reporting of participating funds; the information submitted is not audited, and many analysts believe that the quality of the reporting is tainted and opportunistic. The benefit of the academic study cited here is that the study database was not proscribed by the voluntary participation of funds willing and interested in having their results broadcast beyond their investor base.

What did the study find? The study focussed on determining the "excess return" achieved by the funds. The excess return means the return achieved above the return that would have been expected based on the *Beta* of the fund's portfolio and the performance of the market the beta number is related to. Beta compares movement of a stock relative to the movement of the index or market it is part of.

In other words the study was analysing what is also called "alpha", the measure of the "extra return / extra value provided by the skill of the manager" as opposed to a return that was mainly a product of overall equity market movements. This is what you are paying a hedgie to get for you; positive alpha. Without positive alpha you could save money and just invest your funds in Index ETFs (Exchange Traded Funds) such as the S&P 500 SPY ETF and get what the "market" returns for the year at minimal cost.

In recent years there has been an assumption in the media, popular and financial, that the average excess return achieved by hedgies was in the order of 3–5%, which is meaningful and over time very beneficial to their investors if that excess return is consistently achieved year in and year out. The Clifford study showed that a more accurate estimate of excess return is closer to 5 basis points (5 / 100ths of a %) than 5%. Furthermore the study found:

2004 – 2009 Hedge Fund Quarterly Returns (Total Mean Returns)
10, 126 funds surveyed - Quarterly Return = 1.13%
4,925 funds (out of the 10,126 and those funds that report to data bases such as Tremont) – Quarterly Return = 1.68%
All the other funds (out of the 10,126) = 0.60%
"Dead Funds" (1,083 funds that stopped reporting to data bases) = -0.16%

Not too impressive. It's also worth remembering that the managers of the "Dead Funds" often walked away with enviable base management fees that paid a lot of pumped-up salaries, overheads and entertainment expenses.

Another study that appeared in a book called 'The Hedge Fund Mirage' by Simon Lack produced the following information:

Over the period 1998 through 2010, analysis of 40 large funds (core hedge fund industry participants, not minor aberrations) estimated that:

Cumulative fees in $s earned by the funds = $441 billion

Cumulative profits (net of fees) earned by fund investors = $9 billion

In 2008 and 2009, the effective years of our latest financial crisis and the period that deeply impacted cumulative investor returns for the 1998–2010 period:

Funds earned fees = $83 billion

Decline in / Loss of investor capital = $264 billion

What more needs to be said? It is worth noting that the situation since these stats were generated has actually worsened for hedge funds. The average return over the last two to three years for the hedge fund universe whose performance can be monitored is now less than that of the S&P 500 index.

Here is some information about major hedge fund performance in 2015.

This is a scorecard based on performance data from HSBC, investor updates, and media reports:

Third Point Offshore (Dan Loeb): -4.4% (through September 30)
Pershing Square Holdings (Bill Ackman): -9.6% (performance through October 13)
Marcato International (Mick McGuire): -11.6% (through September 30)
Paulson Advantage (John Paulson): -12% (through September 30)
Omega Overseas Partners (Leon Cooperman): -12.02% (through September 30)
Glenview Capital (Larry Robbins): -13.5% (through September 30)
Greenlight Capital Offshore (David Einhorn): -16.88% (through September 30)
Fortress Macro Fund (Mike Novogratz): -17.49% (fund closing

Courtesy Business Insider UK

Why did these major, historically strong funds underperform?

Overall, two reasons have been put forward, one somewhat theoretical and one factual.

The theoretical argument is that due to a phenomenon referred to as "crowding" (the explosion in hedge fund numbers, now around 10,000 globally) and the fact that many of those funds follow similar trading strategies, the strategies themselves become "crowded". That is, too many participants trying the same tact or trade means the presumed profit for the strategy is competed out and the trade rendered ineffective.

The "market" the strategy is aimed at becomes "efficient" – too many smart, knowledgeable participants acting on the same information competes out the possibility of any extra profit, if any profit at all. It's like an athletic match between two evenly matched opponents, the odds are the game will not end in a rout for the winning side or may just end in a tie.

Second reason is far more egregious than the first. Several big hedge funds invested in the same major trades of the year (Valeant pharmaceuticals of Canada (but also traded on the NYSE) in New York is the prime example. Valeant's share price collapsed by around 80% inflicting super large losses on some of the biggest name funds (Pershing Square, Bill Ackman being a principal victim) and leading to overall losses for the funds.

You might ask, why didn't they use stop losses and limit the pain to 25% for example? Lots of reasons; arrogance, difficulty in exiting big positions without pushing down the share price dramatically, an insistence on staying in the trade because of all the work done in setting it up, self delusion, pride and a desire not to crystallize big losses and loss of face and many others.

Do you think with some work, some discipline and diligence you could achieve excess returns greater than 5 basis points? Not everyone can, but, matching this level of performance isn't quite the same as trying to keep apace of Usain Bolt over 100 meters.

Appendix 10

Fund Managers

Fund managers are, statistically speaking, an easy target all over the world. Study after study, survey after survey, has demonstrated the consistent underperformance of the majority of fund managers. Fund managers do face considerable constraints in managing the assets under their control. Sometimes funds get too big, sometimes the investment charter of the fund requires that it be fully invested in equities at all times, meaning the manager may have no choice but to ride a bear market down, trying to limit the downside as much as he or she can.

Fund managers of mutual funds and unit trusts have to stand ready to redeem shares as well as to issue new shares on a continuing basis. This is not an ideal situation. It means keeping cash reserves you would otherwise like to invest and, particularly in down markets, having to liquidate investments involuntarily when there are usually very high redemption demands from investors. It also means having to invest inflows of new money at times when the manager may see the market as generally over-valued. Fund managers have a bad habit of buying high and selling low, and in some cases do so not because of bad judgment so much as because their fund rules require them to be fully invested at all times. Rules like this are one of the reasons for the growth of hedge-fund-type funds that can act with greater freedom.

There are many successful fund managers who provide above average returns on a consistent basis, but going back again to the bell-shaped curve phenomenon of our universe, those outperformers are, of course, in the minority.

Many fund managers and many pension fund managers aim to "index". That is, they create investment portfolios that mimic major indices such as the Dow, the FTSE, the CAC 40, etc. and hence will perform no better (the aim being literally to perform no worse) than the market in any year. These managers add no "Alpha" to their results. Alpha being a simple statistic – the difference between a fund's return and that achieved either by an index or the average fund with a comparable investment strategy (e.g. growth, equity income, etc.) or the manager's portfolio Beta, a measure of the correlation between the fund and a market index.

Alpha is a measure of the value the manager contributes and creates for his investors, his or her outperformance of the market.

Appendix 11

Day Traders

Defensive Investing is not going to be useful for so-called "day traders". Herodotus, the Greek historian, in speaking about astrology as the state religion of Babylon, said that astrology was "not a religion but a disease of the mind". Day trading is not investing and can literally be or become a disease of the mind.

With the advent of the Internet and Internet trading platforms for equities, currencies, options and futures (spread betting, CFDs (Contract for Difference), etc.) many non-professional traders seeking to either get rich quick or compensate for the loss of mainstream employment became "day traders".

Day trading involves very little in start-up costs and very little effort to organize. You just needed a PC and a trading account with a broker or a so-called spread betting site.

Day traders are so called because they largely seek to turnover their limited financial capital every day in order to try to make a living by trading. Day Traders take very short-term positions ranging from as little as a few minutes to a full trading day. They can and do carry positions overnight but rarely for longer than for a few days.

Many, many day traders have come to grief quickly, many others somewhat more slowly. Few day traders are capable of being anything other than financial gamblers. People who would in days gone by have bet on horses or played lotteries or perhaps visited casinos instead, now with the benefit of PCs and the Internet, are channeled into financial casinos instead.

Most day traders critically lack the education (trading and finance) needed to trade competently, manage their capital and control their risk and find sensible, favorably balanced risk: reward trading opportunities. Day trading is also attractive to compulsive gamblers since it incorporates all the emotional characteristics of gambling including the instant gratification / instant self-flagellation need.

Most people are psychologically / emotionally / behaviorally unsuited to be traders, professional or amateur and day traders wreck themselves upon the shoals of their own ill-suited emotions when trading.

Day trading is a trap for the unwary and self-delusory. Really accomplished, consistently successful traders, trading as part of an organization or for their own account, will tell you that 50% or less of their trades are profitable. It's all about money management and risk management, long hours of market observation, talking markets through with other, knowledgeable traders, back testing trading systems and rigidly controlling your emotions, all the sorts of things the average day trader never does.

And here's one more obstacle to success as a Day Trader. Generally speaking the biggest moves of the day for any stock or index takes place within the first hour of market trading. This means that to have a better chance of making largish, short term gains you need to either carry positions overnight so you're position at market open or you had better get up early, do your research and take your positions in pre-market trading. A real problem here is, unsurprisingly, prices quoted in out-of-hours (exchange trading hours) markets tend to be very extreme with large gaps between bid and offer quotes and the closing "in-hours" price.

Appendix 12

Earning Added Income on Your Portfolio – Selling Covered Call Options

You can generate additional income from your portfolio by selling what are called "covered call options". To do this, you will need an agreement with your broker that allows you to trade options.

Selling a covered call means that once you have bought a stock, you then sell through your broker a call option to another investor. This call option gives that other investor the right to buy the underlying stock from you at the strike price of the call option and within the option duration period that can run from a few weeks to several months plus.

The "covered" aspect of the option means that you own the stock and hence you are not at any price risk in delivering the stock to the investor (your option counterparty who has bought the "call" from you) should it get called because the stock price has risen to or above the option strike price.

When you sell the covered call you will receive the call premium; that is the fee per share that the other investor will pay to you for buying the call from you. The call premium is yours to keep whether the call is ever exercised or not.

Call premiums (the cost to the other investor and what is paid to you) can vary considerably based on the time duration of the call, the stock's historic and estimated volatility and the relation between the strike price of the call and the current price of the underlying stock.

What's the risk?

The risk is foregone profit. If the call is exercised you will receive only the strike price and not the prevailing market price that will always be higher (hence the logic of the other investor exercising the call). You will not lose capital and you will keep the premium and you will get the sale proceeds at the strike price (not the then current, higher price)

What's the benefit?

Writing covered calls generate income similar in a sense to dividend income. If the strike price is not hit, you keep the stock. If the stock price has depreciated since your purchase the call premium received mitigates your loss to some greater or lesser extent.

Note that your broker will not allow you to sell the stock while the call option remains outstanding. This means that, if during the life of the call option, you decide you want to sell the stock (because the price is declining or the company's outlook is poor) you first have to buy back the call, which is quickly and easily done. Typically, when doing this, the value of the call will have decreased if the underlying stock's price has declined. This means that you will, net, end up with a call premium earned of less than that you originally received and would have kept if you had not liquidated the call.

Sounds complicated? Not really. If you're interested there are any number of short, to the point sources of information on covered calls on your broker's website and on many different Internet financial sites.

Why do this?

Principally, for income generation purposes. Covered calls can have a big, positive impact on an investor's portfolio during extended periods of "sideways" moving markets.

A second reason investors do this is that they want to hold the stock over the longer term but want to mitigate any unrealized capital losses if the stock declines by offsetting that price decline with covered call income.

There's a fine balance here. If you want to keep the stock, you're going to sell lower cost "out-of-the-money" call options – options with very high strike prices relative to the stock's current price. These types of options don't cost much and hence don't provide much income. But if you are determined to hold a stock, then any amount of call option income should be satisfactory.

Covered call option selling is not complicated –but I am not suggesting you become an options trader and hence a lot of the theory of options is surplus to your information requirements. Read up on options theory but covered call selling for income is not a trading exercise and hence is reasonably straightforward topic.

Appendix 13

Behavioral Finance

Behavioral Finance is of particular relevance to the process and discipline of Risk Management but the significance of the topic goes well beyond just this aspect of investing.

Behavioral Finance is a discipline that applies the principles of the psychology of human behavior to investing. In part it seeks to analyse and explain stock market movements in terms of human psychology as if the market was in effect a human being.

This approach is entirely reasonable because the stock market, any market, is just an assemblage of human participants and market characteristics and behaviors are formed by the interaction of its participants.

Behavioral Finance examines the behavior of people as investors, their overall relationship with money in general, and again applies the basic principles of the human psyche to analyse why investors, for better and worse, do what they do.

For our purposes I want to review some of the fundamental findings of Behavioral Finance and to talk about why we need to be aware of these principles and our behaviors and how we need to modify and manage them within the context of Defensive Investing and our investment activities.

Behavioral Finance researchers not only observe our investment behavior but, typical of academic psychologists, they run many experiments to try to confirm their various theses about our investment behavior and our overall attitude toward money.

Our behavior as investors is largely inseparable from our overall beliefs, behaviors and psychological outlook. As we interpret the world and act on a daily basis we will act as investors. This can be problematic depending upon on our beliefs, particularly towards money.

The issues we are going to look at in this chapter tie in with the process of making and following Rules. The Rules we make up and strive to follow are a way of controlling our behavior so to avoid the most dysfunctional and self-defeating aspects of our investment behavior. We have some rules for picking stocks and we have and need some rules for our investing actions.

Largely speaking we can divide the key points of Behavioral Finance into:

- How we perceive; and
- How we react.

The perception issues revolve around a tendency to see what we want to see; seeing what accords to our beliefs about ourselves and about how the "market should operate" and what we are *comfortable* perceiving. How we react is a product of what we perceive. If our perception of the market and our own competencies and behaviors are "delusional" then we're largely going to react in a "dysfunctional" manner. Simply translated: we're going to lose money.

Before going further, I want to mention that there are psychologists who specialize in studying and coaching professional traders, such as Ari Kiev, whose books you can read. This speciality has arisen because psychology plays such a fundamental role in the behavior of even the most professional and seasoned traders. There is also a cadre of therapists and psychiatrists who specialize in financial industry patients, a lucrative practice.

Let's start with how we act and react to investment events. Not surprisingly, Behavioral Finance advocates will generally say that greed and fear are the two most prominent motives in shaping our investment behavior.

Greed

Greed is what prevents us from making rational investment decisions from the outset regarding what we invest in. And continues through the process of managing our investments – how to manage risk, when to sell. Greed is the force that motivates us to try to get rich quick, get rich the easy way and I suppose keep up or catch up with other people whom we think are better off than we are. Greed is not good, despite what Gordon Gekko once said. It doesn't "clarify" our thinking or behavior; it subverts it, because it is an irrational and very powerful emotion.

In the 19th century Nathan Rothschild, when asked about the secret to his investment success, said "I always leave the last penny of profit to the next fellow". What that means is selling when you reasonably think an investment has topped-out rather than greedily clinging on for "more", only to find your investment then failing and you losing money. There are tools other than intuition or sentiment you can use to develop some simple rules for curbing self-defeating greed.

How do you this? It's relatively simple, mechanically and we've explored this process in depth in Chapter 3 on Risk Management, but in brief:

1 Use trailing stops, as the price of your investment rises your stop-loss point rises concomitantly. The great greed-defeating value of this simple tool is that it is entirely mechanical. Once you set it, you should leave it (you could always tighten it, but never enlarge it – that's greed getting the better of you). Once you set your automatic stop, you have taken the emotion out of the exit decision.

2 As an alternative (but always with the use of stop loss points, preferably set with your broker rather than mental stops), set a target upside price that you reasonably think an investment can reach and, if reached, sell half of your investment and take that part of the profit and run with the remainder. This is harder because it necessitates forming a somewhat specific idea of what that price peak will be.

3 A common saying among traders is that the market will always give you another chance (another chance to lose as well as make money). What this means is that if you miss out on an investment or you exit before a share's price peak, another opportunity will almost always arise for you to re-invest in that particular stock or fund or some comparable investment. Professional investors do this all the time. If the opportunity doesn't present itself in a specific stock then it will over time in some other share. You don't have to be greedy; you don't have to suffer "post-decisional regret".

Fear

The fear of losing and of realizing losses is the other critical emotion that undermines investors and most particularly traders with their shorter time horizons. Fear of losing is what stops investors from cutting their losses and running their profits. Fear of losing is what stops investors from using stop-loss points below their buying price and for causing people to double up / average down: that is, buying additional exposure to losing positions in the hope of making it back by having reduced your cost basis (average price). This kind of behavior is wholly irrational. Why? Because if you do not control your downside risk, and do not cut your losses but, not only let them run and then increase your exposure, you are almost certain to lose all your capital over time. A common stock market saying is "don't try to catch falling knives (falling shares)"

Doubling down, averaging down, is a sure-fire loser. It is self-defeating and self-punishing to an extreme. A trader's psychologist will tell you that in many instances this behavior is all about lacking self-worth and wanting to punish yourself for some deep-seated inadequacies you believe you have.

Fear is also what makes traders cut their profits. The trading floors of the major commodities and derivatives exchanges are full of individual traders who waste their energy, and ultimately their lives, taking 1% and 2% gains alongside their 1% and 2% losses. Their downside tendencies are fine in principle but their attitude to managing gains is entirely self-defeating. You cannot succeed and build capital by being fearful and just "scalping" tiny gains.

Again, the key point to take away from this brief discussion about fear and greed is to use our Risk Management techniques to separate your trading behavior from your emotions. Controlling our emotions and managing our behaviors is something we can all try to do, and to some greater or lesser extent succeed at.

Successfully altering our emotions may take 25 years of Freudian analysis and this can be of value. But short of having that kind of time available, we just need to follow mechanical solutions to override our emotions. I'm not suggesting that's easy, but doing so is a learning process wholly akin to learning how to play tennis or bridge or basic do-it-yourself techniques. We can carry all sorts of emotional baggage and still learn to volley a tennis ball. The same is true of rational, functional and proven investment mechanics.

The issue of perception

Behavioral Finance by observation and experimentation has found that not surprisingly we're pretty good at deluding ourselves when it comes to money and investing issues. In doing so, we set all sorts of traps for ourselves, for example:

- We minimize our perception of the losses we've incurred and overstate our gains, thus building a false sense of competence. As a result, we repeat the same investment mistakes because we won't recognize them.
- We tend to exaggerate in our own minds the importance of both good and bad company and stock market news and events, and we tend to place too much importance on the most recent news rather than critical company or market trends.
- Behavioral Finance practitioners believe that this is one of the main reasons stocks and markets get undervalued or overvalued. We become dangerously over-optimistic about the magnitude of stock or market gains and fail to see the possibilities of recovery in stock prices because we become unreasonably pessimistic.
- We fail to interpret events objectively. We believe what we want to believe about a stock, a market tipster, economic and political events because our beliefs make us comfortable and we like to have them confirmed. We interpret events as always conforming to our beliefs and hence we don't make objective analyses and judgements.
    - A common example of this point is accepting as valid only the points and recommendations of people (analysts, brokers, friends, other investors) who have the same belief system we do. We don't listen to contrarian views and hence have no checks and balances in place for reality testing our own beliefs and behaviors.
    - Using these types of checks and balances can be uncomfortable, but listening to, and as importantly, weighing contrarian views can be a tremendously effective tool.

Let's set out some Behavioral Finance rules for ourselves and then let's follow them as consistently as we can:

1. **Always use risk management techniques**
   a. Always set stop losses and if your broker's system accepts trailing stops do the "easy" and I believe sensible and effective thing and use them
   b. If you do this then you immediately have put yourself in control of and beyond harm from most of the pain of greed and fear in investing.
   c. Put your stops in right after you're brokerage account is credited with a purchase. Don't postpone, you'll either procrastinate for emotive reasons or just forget about doing it.
2. **Make it a habit to seek out and objectively consider all market viewpoints and bits of information**
   a. Reality test your views – investing is not a religious faith issue, the point is to be correct in your investment decisions not to adhere to the death to the "faith of your fathers". Reality testing your views is the "professional investor" thing to do – it's better to be wise and knowledgeable about the market than to be "vaingloriously right" in your smug, tunnel-vision views. Taking on board alternative views and strategies complicates life but it also enriches it and enriches us.
   b. Use the information you gather to develop simple "what if?" scenarios. What if the other guy is right? You need to manage your risk and you want to prepare effective actions just in case that other guy's thesis is correct. Compare their "what ifs" to yours. What is the risk: reward balance between their views playing out versus your views? If you do this, you can evolve a useable idea as to where you should position yourself in investment

terms and how to do that based on the tools this book provides you with.

3 **Evaluate yourself and your performance**

a In the privacy of your own home, keep tally of your performance, every trade as well as the value of your investment accounts, and review what you've done well and what you've done not so well. The point of the self-review is to learn – don't beat yourself up, stick to the main point. Did you do what you felt was right and reasonable? Did you manage your risk? What decisions did you take that just weren't in accord with the market as it developed? What outcomes were really beyond your control, such as "events", company specific or market wide?

b Remember that you have the time and tools to evolve and implement better decisions and investment management processes and doing that is half of the challenge and half the reward.

c Check to see what professional investors have done. Check hedge fund stats and mutual fund performance. You may find that what you thought to be disappointing performance on your part was not very different from that of mainstream professional investors. The point here is not to make yourself feel better about being as mediocre as your benchmark, but rather to give you a realistic context of how you're doing. You can be sure that professional investors, either on their own initiative or that of their bosses or clients, are also reviewing their performance and analysing how to do things better.

NB. You can check hedge fund results by receiving free monthly hedge fund results tables from sites such as www.hedgeindex.com. You can check mutual fund /

investment trust performance from any number of websites such as Yahoo Finance, your own broker, *Money Observer* magazine (UK), Investors Chronicle's website and so on.

Record keeping and performance reviews can be a bore. It doesn't have to be done excessively or constantly, but without doing at least monthly reviews, Behavioral Finance demonstrates conclusively in study after study our ability to delude ourselves about our actual performance. Our tendency to self-delusion is unrelated to demography. It doesn't matter how well educated you are, where you were born or what your father did for a living.

4 **If you are fearful or feel indecisive**

a Do nothing for a while. You may be indecisive because there just isn't useful information available about specific stocks or industries or themes or the market to serve as a firm basis for taking decisions.

b If you're fearful, don't trade: no professional trader or investor would do so while not in control of their emotions. We can talk about being frozen with fear, immobilized by fear, it happens. But one way to escape is to recognize and to consciously decide not to act until we can overcome our fear. We then have to try to overcome our fear, but by pressuring ourselves to act when we can't sensibly do so only exacerbates the problem.

The Efficient Market Hypothesis

As you may be aware there is a stock market theory known as the Efficient Market Hypothesis. As defined by Wikipedia:

"In finance, the efficient-market hypothesis (EMH) asserts that financial markets are 'informationally efficient'. That is, one cannot consistently achieve returns in excess of average market returns on a risk-adjusted basis, given the information available at the time the investment is made.

"There are three major versions of the hypothesis: 'weak', 'semi-strong' and 'strong'. The weak-form EMH claims that prices on traded assets (*e.g.*, stocks, bonds, or property) already reflect all past publicly available information. The semi-strong-form of EMH claims both that prices reflect all publicly available information and that prices instantly change to reflect new public information. The strong-form EMH additionally claims that prices instantly reflect even hidden or 'insider' information. There is evidence for and against the weak form and semi-strong-form EMHs, while there is lots of evidence against strong-form EMH."

Exponents of Behavioral Finance unsurprisingly reject the validity of the Efficient Market Hypothesis on the basis of both theory and observation.

Theoretically, how can the market be efficient given that is just a kind of clearing-house of human financial behavior? Knowing what we know about human behavior in general and what Behavioral Finance researchers have found with regard to human financial behavior specifically, how can a collective of irrational actors be rational and hence efficient?

Observationally, it is a fact that there are a number of investors (albeit limited in number) that do outperform the market on a fairly consistent basis (with enough consistency to minimize mere luck or statistical probability).

The EMH looks good on paper but is tough to put into practice and does not consistently produce the result predicted by the theory. I do not want in any way to denigrate academic financial research or its output. A lot of useful material has been produced by academics in economics and finance, but an awful lot with regard to the utility of the research output turns on finding ways to practically employ that research.

Economics is not a science of immutable laws, it's a social science and it is predicated on the concept of what the "rational man" would do in economic terms. Well, for many of us, things start looking dire with regard to economics or any field of study that is predicated on consistently rational human behavior.

Common behavioral traps

Set out below is an excerpt from Paul Farrell's excellent column on Marketwatch.com – Farrell, ex-Wall Street and now a financial journalist, is himself an advocate of Behavioral Finance.

> **Overconfidence bias:** You love trading and gambling. You pay little attention to the fees, commissions and taxes, because you know you'll score big.
>
> **Blinders:** Investors often stereotype certain companies, stocks and funds as "winners" or "losers" (Dell? Apple?), often missing turning points signaling a change in company fortunes, opportunities and reversals.
>
> **Heroics:** Irrational investors tend to overestimate their stock-picking abilities, underestimate Mr. Market. Then later exaggerate their successes, talk about the one that got away.
>
> **Denial:** Once locked in, irrational investors hate admitting they've made a bad decision. It's an ego thing. So they hang on to losers, even refuse to sell losers. It's un-American. Or means you're not as manly or as smart as you thought.
>
> **Attachment bias**: You fall in love with "special" stocks. You exaggerate virtues, downplay problems and then hold on too long.
>
> **Extremism bias:** Irrational investors have trouble assessing risk, often bet big, and lose big. Probable events become certain. Unlikely events become impossible. So you're likely to miscalculate your risks.

Anchors: In your mind you tend lock in price targets, like a hundred-buck stock or Dow 15,000, and then minimize any data that suggests you're wrong.

Ownership bias: Once purchased, you value what's yours even higher, like overvaluing your home. That blinds you to the real value, adds to your losses.

Herd mentality: For all the talk about macho individuality, the truth is, most investors don't think for themselves and tend to follow the crowd, or blindly track some trend.

Getting-even bias: You lose, and then you try to break even taking extra risk, doubling-down. You get overanxious, overreact, and you lose more.

Small-numbers bias: Making decisions on limited data that's incomplete and likely exaggerated.

Loss aversion: Many cautious people tend to avoid losses more than seek gains. That fear keeps investors out of the market too long, and in "safe" money markets.

Pride: You hate selling losers, hate admitting error. You have a no-talk rule.

Risk averse: You take too little risk after a big loss or a losing streak, get too conservative, don't trust yourself, and miss opportunities for higher returns.

Myopic bias: You think recent data's more important than older information. So you may pull back after a losing streak, or ride a winning streak till you lose it.

Cognitive dissonance: You filter out bad news and tend to ignore and discard new information that conflicts with your biases, preconceptions and belief system.

Bandwagon: You disregard fundamentals. You think you understand "momentum." You conclude that "so many" followers can't possibly be wrong.

Confirmation: You're not only critical of any news that contradicts your beliefs; you blindly accept any data that confirms beliefs.

Rationalization: You are super logical and can marshal lots of evidence to back up whatever you first decide to buy, even if it's based on limited logic and data.

Anchoring bias: You rely too much on readily available data, just because it's available, even when you know it could be faulty.

House money: You treat winnings as if they belong to the house or casino. Then you take bigger risks, giving it all back, and then some.

Disposition effect: You tend to lock in gains and hang onto losses, selling shares in an up market, hanging onto losers too long, similar to loss aversion.

Outcome bias: You judge your decisions on results rather than the context when the decision was made. That'll result in misleading you the next time.

Sunk costs bias: You treat money already invested in a stock as more valuable than future opportunities, so you often hang on rather than sell and reinvest.

Perfect behavioral storm: Separately, each bias is bad enough. Combined, they become bubbles, set you and wipe you out. Either way, quants and behaviorists can easily manipulate you into what they want, blowing bubbles and popping them without you ever knowing what's happening ... manipulating you like a mindless puppet.

See the chart below from the *Investors Chronicle* that neatly summarizes many common behavioral mistakes and the errors they result in.

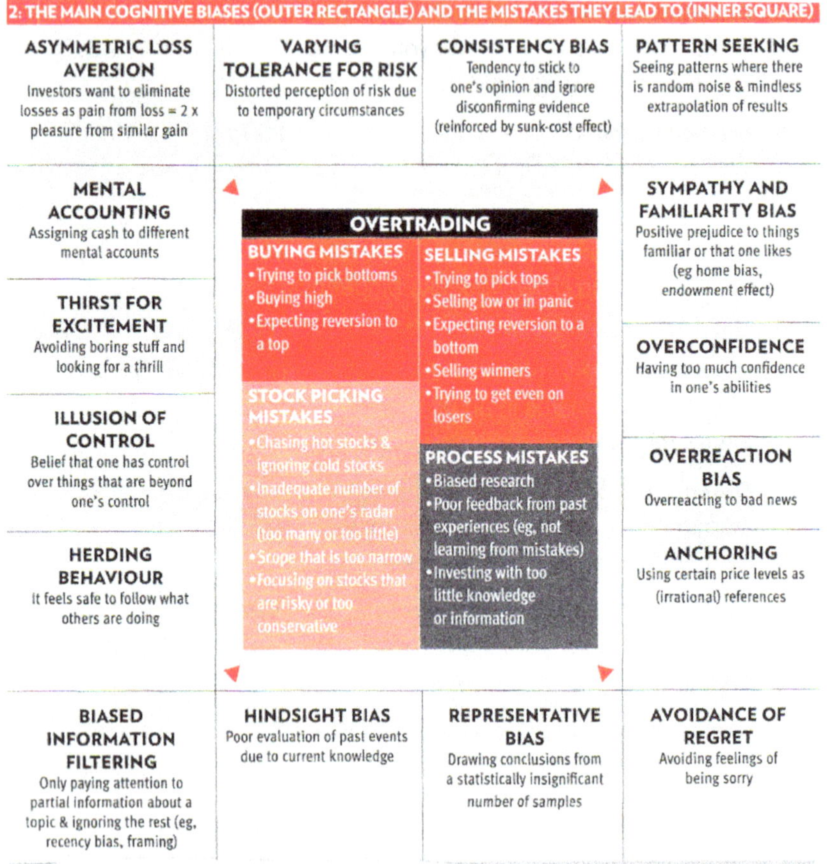

2: THE MAIN COGNITIVE BIASES (OUTER RECTANGLE) AND THE MISTAKES THEY LEAD TO (INNER SQUARE)
ASYMMETRIC LOSS AVERSION
Investors want to eliminate losses as pain from loss = 2 x pleasure from similar gain
VARYING TOLERANCE FOR RISK
Distorted perception of risk due to temporary circumstances
CONSISTENCY BIAS
Tendency to stick to one's opinion and ignore disconfirming evidence (reinforced by sunk-cost effect)
PATTERN SEEKING
Seeing patterns where there is random noise & mindless extrapolation of results
MENTAL ACCOUNTING
Assigning cash to different mental accounts
THIRST FOR EXCITEMENT
Avoiding boring stuff and looking for a thrill
ILLUSION OF CONTROL
Belief that one has control over things that are beyond one's control
HERDING BEHAVIOUR
It feels safe to follow what others are doing
OVERTRADING
BUYING MISTAKES
•Trying to pick bottoms
•Buying high
•Expecting reversion to a top
SELLING MISTAKES
•Trying to pick tops
•Selling low or in panic
•Expecting reversion to a bottom
•Selling winners
•Trying to get even on losers
STOCK PICKING MISTAKES
•Chasing hot stocks & ignoring cold stocks
•Inadequate number of stocks on one's radar (too many or too little)
•Scope that is too narrow
•Focusing on stocks that are risky or too conservative
PROCESS MISTAKES
•Biased research
•Poor feedback from past experiences (eg, not learning from mistakes)
•Investing with too little knowledge or information
SYMPATHY AND FAMILIARITY BIAS
Positive prejudice to things familiar or that one likes (eg home bias, endowment effect)
OVERCONFIDENCE
Having too much confidence in one's abilities
OVERREACTION BIAS
Overreacting to bad news
ANCHORING
Using certain price levels as (irrational) references
BIASED INFORMATION FILTERING
Only paying attention to partial information about a topic & ignoring the rest (eg, recency bias, framing)
HINDSIGHT BIAS
Poor evaluation of past events due to current knowledge
REPRESENTATIVE BIAS
Drawing conclusions from a statistically insignificant number of samples
AVOIDANCE OF REGRET
Avoiding feelings of being sorry

Courtesy of Investors Chronicle/ FT Publications

Trading and, to a somewhat lesser extent, investing, is a lot like gambling in that they involve and invoke many of the same emotions; greed, self-worth and fear of loss (of money, status and self-image). Trading, like gambling, is often tragically underpinned and motivated by a desire for self-inflicted punishment and self-destruction. Traders, like gamblers, can have all sorts of superstitions to support their trading activities.

Really successful traders (and by the way there is a series of books on "trading wizards" that is worth reading) tend to embody behaviors that are million miles away from that of the "typical" amateur trader and day trader. They are very focused on the goal of not losing money and **not losing money and not losing money.** They may well enjoy the occasional adrenalin rush of trading, they may enjoy the "contest", the daily evaluation of what they've done but...they are also rational, they focus on risk management and they spend hours reviewing their trading activities, doing research and plotting trading strategies.

Some writers such as Paul Farrell tell us that we will never overcome the limitations of human financial behavior and hence will always fall into one behavioral trap or another as investors.

A bit fatalistic perhaps, but probably pretty accurate in general.

The best we can do as investors is to be aware of the common behavioral traps and to try really hard and consistently to review our behavior and eschew getting caught by these traps.

Let's review more behavioral traps to avoid:

1 Thinking we're expert if we've had some investment successes. This is always dangerous because it's almost always wrong, it leads to complacency and laxity in risk management and it is a step down the road of persistent self-delusion

2 Mistaking being carried by a bull market for investment acumen. Try always to distinguish between gains that are product of a "rising tide carrying all boats" from the product of our own intellect and action. This point clearly relates to point 1 made above, but the result of a bull market tide

can cause us to think that we now have clear and objective confirmation of our skill. We don't. We can analyze what's happened, what we did and draw lessons. We will find that from time to time we do exercise skill and good judgment, but we need to know the practical limits.

3 **Greed.** Beyond moral issues, greed is a compulsion that distorts judgment and hence behavior and outcomes. Do what Nathaniel Rothschild did – "leave the last penny of profit to other fellow". It worked well for him!

How do you deal with greed? You set exit points for your investments. When a price target you have set is reached either you;

a Sell 50% of your position, you'll never go broke taking a profit;

b Put tight stops under your remaining position;

c If the stock's / the company's performance changes for the worse post your 50% sell the remainder and take your remaining profit.

The answer to almost every financial behavioral problem is **mechanical / process driven.** Have a plan, have stops, have targets and stick to them, because we'll never stop being human and falling prey to behavioral traps if we don't set mechanisms for sidestepping them.

4 **Perception issues.** In this short review of some of the key principals of Behavioral Finance, the last group of issues I want to deal with are various perception problems that we face.

a **Filtering.** We see and interpret all data through the screen, the filter of our prejudices, no matter how we developed our prejudices. A lot of "filtering" has an emotional basis and so can be very strong, very resistant and hard to overcome. A lot of the underlying emotion is the product of fears. Again, the practical solution to the problem is to develop a habit of wanting to hear the views of others and views that are contrary to our beliefs.

i. Some readers may be familiar with "neuro-linguistic programming" a common therapy and behavioral change process, where we work at making things we normally don't like into positives in our mind so that we do what's necessary and best for ourselves. NLP isn't easy but it can be a practical way of making some useful behavioral alterations.

b **Recency.** This is the perceptual phenomenon of putting too much reliance, too much value and credence of our most recent observations, ideas, perceptions, advice received. It's that tendency to follow the "last, best idea" we've heard.

i. We need balance in analyzing information and to need to review more than just the most recent information we have. We need to look at information when possible from different angles.

ii. There is a value to recent information, "things" change, trends alter direction and recent action and information has value but … like all information and trends, it can be transitory and putting that information into a larger, longer-term context can give us a basis for evaluating the quality of that recent information.

c **Normalcy.** Normalcy is the desire we have for things to be "as they've been". The desire we have, the belief we develop that if something, such as a stock price, has changed for the worse recently, it will revert back to the previous "better condition". Things will get back "normal" and normal is whatever "good" thing we previously experienced.

In stock market terms the normalcy trap is very common in the face of prolonged bear markets. For example, NASDAQ post 2001 and the belief that those investors who didn't get out that market and reinvest the proceeds in sectors that rose, held that the market would return to "normal", would return to the rapid and dramatic price rises experienced in the late '90s, thus covering their grievous losses.

The problem with "normalcy" is that it entraps us into inaction and wishful thinking and prevents us from developing sensible strategies to improve our investment performance.

How to deal with "normalcy"? Be aware of the problem and try to make non-emotive, reasonably objective analyses of the situation you're confronting.

Consider this:

- We've lost 20% on our investment in a Nasdaq Index fund. What are out options?
    - Keep our position:
        - Hope for a return to "normalcy" – the pre-2001 situation of dramatic price rises and so recoup our losses and prosper
        - Potentially worsen our losses by not cutting them and falling into the normalcy trap
    - Sell our position:
        - Cut our loss, as painful as that may be
        - Re-invest the proceeds in another sector fund where there is objective evidence of recovery and upward momentum (value stocks made a

big post tech boom / bust come back post 2001), thus recouping our losses

Regardless of the eventual outcomes, which of course we cannot know in advance, what strikes me about the above argument is: which course of action sounds "rational" and which sounds potentially self-deluding? At the time a decision needs to be made, should be made, which course of action eschews emotion and seems to have objectivity?

The emotion of "Keep our position" is fear of loss. "Reversion to Normalcy" facilitates the delusion that we can escape the pain of loss by holding on for a return to normalcy.

Again, dealing with these common behavioral traps isn't easy. But for most of us, even the more emotional, if we take the time to review in our own minds our possible motivations, our possible courses of action, and if we implement good risk management consistently we can mitigate the impact of these traps.

More views on investment behavior

Now read through the web article below, excerpted from the 'Rude Awakening' website.

Rude Awakening Pro

July 13, 2015

How One Chart Can More Than Double Your Trading Gains

Think inside the box

The meat of the move

Plus: Throwing good money after bad...

By Greg Guenthner

Think outside the box?

Forget it. If you want the chance to double your trading *gains*, you need to think inside the box...

So here's the deal: If you follow the chart I'm about to reveal, you'll have the opportunity to drastically *improve your trading results.* Permanently.

Don't worry… you don't need to know a thing about technical analysis. You don't have to interpret confusing indicators. And it's so simple not even Hillary Clinton could play dumb. Think "inside the box" and I guarantee you'll see results...

Best of all, thinking inside the box works for any timeframe. Your investing horizon doesn't matter one bit. You could be looking at a weekly chart, a daily, or even a 30-minute chart.

Alright, so here's the chart that'll renew your faith in trading:

I want you to focus on the area inside the red box. It contains the "meat" of this stock's jump from $45 to $90. The name of the stock and the time frame aren't important here.

Some move, huh? But dollars to donuts, I bet most traders playing this stock didn't book the 55% gain you see inside the box.

Why not?

Because most traders get greedy. It's that simple. They want to squeeze every last ounce of profit out of the stock. They're not content grabbing the strongest, most predictable gains found within the box.

In this example, the trader wants in at $45 when this stock begins exploding higher. And he wants to exit at its absolute peak near $90 for a clean double.

OK, newsflash, pal: Getting out at the exact top is as rare as a pink unicorn. It hardly happens—if ever. Sure, it's easy to play Monday morning quarterback and say you would've sold at the top. But when you're intoxicated by the prospect of triple-digit gains? Please…

Let's say our trading friend buys this stock near $45, right as the stock crosses into the red box. The market proves his analysis correct as the stock takes off. He feels like Gordon Gekko…

Fast-forward a few weeks and our trader's sitting on a double when the stock rockets to $90. Pure genius, right?

Right. But the stock's smashing performance has got him so full of himself he can't think straight. Greed kicks in. He becomes obsessed. And instead of diligently planning his exit, he's thinking about turning his double into a triple...

Then the stock slips on a banana peel, and suddenly it's at $75. Then it takes an even bigger hit, dropping below $65. Now what, genius?

But instead of selling, our friend wants to wait it out. He thinks he's got a tiger by the tail, he's convinced his thesis is correct and the stock will be back to $90 lickety-split.

So his reasoning turns from hopeful to downright *irrational before he knows what hit him…*

If it could just get back to $90 — then I'll sell.

If only! That's exactly the kind of thinking that turns big winners into average trades… or worse.

As the stock continues dropping he finally wants out. So he sells his shares in a panic as the stock finally dips back into the $50-range.

He ended up selling just a few dollars higher than his purchase price for less than a 20% gain. Nothing to scoff at—but not the 50-something percent he could have made with a plan.

Our tragicomic trader was looking for home-run gains. Now he's stuck with a meaningless single up the *middle.*

That's why you have to think – and trade – inside the box. That means limiting your expectations to the middle range of a stock's major move. You'll never get rich guessing when a falling stock will bounce. Or when it'll peak. "Thinking inside the box" takes all the guesswork out of it…

If you patiently wait for a stock to break above resistance you have a chance at riding a major move like the one shown here. And if you “think inside the box” you don’t need hope. No guesswork, no hunches. Just the facts, ma’am.

So if you’ve got a winning stock like this that loses momentum, set a stop-loss just below the final leg of the big move. In this case, a tad below $75. (Take another look at the chart). Once the stock falls back into the trading box, dump the sucker. In our example, that would have turned a mediocre, frustrating trade into a big winner.

So next time you’re about to trade a stock breaking out above resistance levels, remember to keep your sights inside the red box. Do*n’t g*et greedy. Stick with your trailing stops. And never play catch-up.

Trading “inside the box” will make a world of difference. You’ll see th*e results when you tally your profits* every month...

So start thinking inside the box.

Lastly, read the following article taken from the ‘Seeking Alpha’ website, a daily compendium of stock, bond and commodity market articles independently authored by a wide range of writers.

Zen And The Art Of Investing

Jul. 13, 2015 6:56 PM ET

Summary

- Reduce feelings of fear and greed by redefining what “making money” means.
- Limit investment frequency to fixed intervals to avoid obsessing over stock prices.
- Spend less than you earn, and compare your performance to nothing and nobody.

Most people accept the notion that emotions such as fear or greed undermine rational judgment, and contribute to typical investment mistakes such as buying high and selling low. While we enjoy the thrill and satisfaction of exciting and rapidly profitable stock investments, most of us are (or will soon become) only too familiar with how quickly and unpredictably those feelings give way to frustration, anger, humiliation and sometimes even outright terror. Avoiding all emotional attachments to money would probably help most of us earn it and keep it more efficiently, and would also simply help us enjoy life a bit more.

The problem is that most people can't just simply flip a switch to make themselves more emotionally detached when it comes to investing. The simple fact is that making money is fun, and losing money, not so much. One solution, though, is to redefine what "making money" or "losing money" actually means, and to adopt an investment process where you're almost always "making money" regardless of market conditions and stock prices.

To the majority of investors, "making money" means that the price of their stock investments is up. "Losing money" means the price of their stock investments is going down. If that's the definition that you use, then gyrating stock prices will naturally cause you to feel emotions such as fear and greed. You're watching your net worth flit this way and that, and the complete lack of control and foresight that you have over stock prices will only exacerbate those feelings of fear and greed – unless you can delude yourself into thinking you can predict and control stock prices. In time, powerful feelings of fear and greed may steer you towards poor investment decisions – panic selling, or buying stocks simply because the price is rocketing higher. And at some point, you may well find yourself discretely checking stock prices on your smartphone while you're on vacation or reading your kids a bedtime story. At that point, you can be certain that your investments are destroying your quality of life when they should be enhancing it.

My solution to the problems of emotional investing is that I don't define "making money" or "losing money" based on the price of my portfolio. Instead, I define "making money" as "spending less than I earn." I have adopted an entire investment process based on that definition. To see whether I am making money or losing money, I follow three discrete steps.

First, I use a spreadsheet to keep careful track of my average monthly expenses, and how those expenses increase or decrease over time.

Second, I list all of my stock positions and other passive income sources on the same spreadsheet. I include the annual dividend information and number of shares for each position, as well as the historical average dividend growth rate. This produces a good estimate of the total dividend, interest and rental income I should expect each month.

Third, exactly once a month (never more and never less frequently), I subtract my actual expenses from my actual income, and then I invest whatever is leftover into more income-producing assets. I will add the new positions I bought into the spreadsheet, and will also take the time to update the spreadsheet for any new dividend announcements or revisions to my probable future spending.

I invest my savings once a month regardless of market conditions, and regardless of whether I can find a bargain or not. I find the best companies I can trading at the best prices available, but I don't wait for better prices because I can't predict or control if or when I will ever find any. I have decided that since I can't predict or control stock prices, stock prices will be irrelevant to my process of investing once a month. I have far less anxiety now that I have made a conscious choice to remove that layer of uncertainty of whether I should or shouldn't invest now, or later, or based on conditions I can't predict or change.

But beyond my choice to invest regardless of market conditions, there is a more mathematical reason why investing carries little emotional impact for me. The reason why is because most of the time, the first thing I see at the end of each month when I reinvest my savings is that my annual income will have gone up, simply because I've bought more income producing assets. It's a small enough change to my annual income that I find it satisfying and constructive, but not electrifying. One of my main sources of satisfaction, though, is that I have a good deal of control over how much I spend. Much of the income growth I see has to do with choices I can foresee and manage – as opposed to random gyrations of share prices, which I don't even try to predict.

But that's not the only source of the monthly income raises I earn. I mainly own shares of companies with very long track records for raising dividends. I take the time each month to update my spreadsheet for new dividend announcements – more often than not, new dividend increases. I can't control when, whether or by how much companies will raise dividends, obviously, so I see it as an added surprise bonus when they do. It's rare to see dividend cuts with the companies I own, but even when it does happen, the impact is relatively small since my income sources are highly diversified.

One feature of my investment process is that almost every month, my annual income goes up regardless of whether the stock market is up or down. What's important about this is that from my perspective, I'm almost always "making money" each month, spending less than I earn, and it is unusual that I end up "losing money" in any given month. That's why I don't experience sensations of fear when it comes to investing.

But as far as greed goes, I have to admit that my process does allow for it to slip in from time to time. The reason why is that my spreadsheet plugs in the historical average dividend growth rates and my average savings rates, and projects my dividend income in ten-, twenty-, thirty-, forty- and fifty-year time horizons. What I've found is that even buying a small number of shares each month may add only a trickle to my annual income, but will translate into enormous income gains in the future. It's not an entirely emotion-free process, but I find that there is a big difference between the feeling of greed you get from a source of immediate gratification (like from a surging stock price of a company you own), and the multi-decade greed you feel when you see the benefits of spending less than you earn. Multi-decade greed feels more virtuous, and doesn't come with an endorphin high.

Stock prices are not entirely irrelevant to me. When the end of the month comes, and I pay my bills and see how much income is left over to invest, I check prices for stocks that I am considering to buy for my portfolio. Oftentimes, I add shares of companies that I already own, and the price for those shares is sometimes down from the month before. But what other investors might see as a "loss" on their portfolio, I see as an opportunity to buy more shares at a higher yield, and thereby grow my future portfolio income that much faster. The harder the stock market drops, the better off my future income is going to be, so long as I keep saving money each month and buying more shares. Under my investment approach, there's positively no financial reason at all to feel fear when prices are falling – and I don't. If anything, it's when I see falling prices that sensations of greed might start to prickle at the back of my neck. And if the stock market rallies and I end up having to pay top dollar for the investments I make at the end of the month, I still see my future income going up (albeit at a slower rate). That's nothing to become despondent about, but is certainly less reason to be giddy with greed. Emotionally speaking, wherever stock prices go, it's a win win situation under my investment process.

There are a few things my investment process explicitly does NOT include. I almost never sell anything once I've bought it. I don't spend principal. I don't check stock prices on my smartphone unless doing so is relevant to my process (that is, unless it's the end of the month and I'm in the market to invest my savings). I don't track my portfolio's price performance, or compare it to other benchmarks. Why would I? Being able to reliably spend less than you earn is a binary condition – a wider margin is nice, but ultimately irrelevant in your day-to-day life. And if you can spend less than you earn, then it's entirely irrelevant whether some other investor or group of investors is doing better or worse than you. I'd say the same is true if you have a definite trajectory for reaching the point where your portfolio income and other income sources will support your lifestyle. An investment process such as the one I describe would enable any investor to track exactly when his or her portfolio will churn out the required number, and with consistent savings and dividend increases, that time period will only grow shorter and shorter – completely independent of where the stock market may or may not go.

Would my process work for everyone? No. It probably works best for investors who wish to live entirely off portfolio income (or a combination of portfolio income, salary, pensions, rents and other income). My process probably works best for investors who are inclined to invest in companies or funds that pay stable, and preferably growing, dividends. My process may or may not work for investors who are mandated to outperform particular benchmarks – I couldn't tell you. My purpose is not to describe a universal process that works for everyone, but to illustrate how an investor might go about defining their own goals and designing their own investment process in a way that reduces stress and the manages emotional peaks and troughs. I'd be interested in hearing any examples of other investment processes that other readers use, and how effective those processes have been.

Excerpt from Rude Trader Pro, June, 2016

www.ingramcontent.com/pod-product-compliance
Lightning Source LLC
Chambersburg PA
CBHW070350200326
41518CB00012B/2195
9781907720215